COWLEY PUBLICATIONS is a ministry of the brothers of the Society of Saint John the Evangelist, a monastic order in the Episcopal Church. Our mission is to provide books and resources for those seeking spiritual and theological formation. Cowley Publications is committed to developing a new generation of writers and teachers who will encourage people to think and pray in new ways about spirituality, reconciliation, and the future.

T0159342

Disclosures

Conversations Gay and Spiritual

Michael Ford

COWLEY PUBLICATIONS
Cambridge, Massachusetts

Published in the United States of America by Cowley Publications, a division of the Society of Saint John the Evangelist. No portion of this book may be reproduced, stored in or introduced into a retrieval system, or transmitted, in any form or by any means—including photocopying—without the prior written permission of Cowley Publications, except in the case of brief quotations embedded in critical articles and reviews.

Published by Darton, Longman and Todd, London UK, 2004
Copyright © 2004 Michael Ford

Library of Congress Cataloging-in-Publication Data

Ford, Michael, 1956–
    Disclosures : conversations gay and spiritual / Michael Ford.
        p. cm.
    Includes bibliographical references.
    ISBN 1-56101-228-9 (pbk. : alk. paper) 1. Christian gays—Religious
life. 2. Homosexuality—Religious aspects—Christianity. I. Title.
    BV4596.G38F67 2005
    261.8'35766—dc22   2005008288

Cover design: Gary Ragaglia

This book was printed in the United States of America on acid-free paper.

Cowley Publications
4 Brattle Street
Cambridge, Massachusetts 02138
800-225-1534 • www.cowley.org

For
Sister Eva Heymann SHCJ

*To discriminate against our sisters and brothers
who are lesbian or gay, on grounds of their sexual orientation,
for me is as totally unacceptable and unjust
as apartheid ever was.*

ARCHBISHOP DESMOND TUTU
SOUTHWARK CATHEDRAL, 2004

Contents

Prelude 9

1   Heart and Soul 35
2   Beyond Words 45
3   Saints and Shepherds 57
4   Guarded Secrets 63
5   Through the Whispering Darkness 69
6   Madness and Passion 77
7   Ages of Mystery 87
8   Hunted 93
9   Masks of Compassion 99
10 Terminal Loneliness 105
11 The Wedding Veil 111
12 Noontide 115
13 A Song of Liberation 121
14 Maternal Instincts 127
15 Greek Fire 133
16 Intimacy and Distance 137
17 Unholy Orders 143
18 A Daring Confidence 151
19 Light and Shade 159
20 Master of Disguise 165
21 Out of the Wilderness 171
22 The Inner Voice of Truth 177
23 The Long Search 183
24 On Being a Person 191
25 The Beat of a Different Drum 197
26 A Gay Priest in Hollywood 203
    Finale: A Symphony of Love 211

Notes 215

Prelude

This is an invitation to enter the spiritual and psychological lives of gay people from a variety of denominations on three continents at a time when homosexuality is proving to be one of the most divisive issues in the history of modern Christianity. It is the first opportunity many have had to articulate their experiences for a wider audience and a few are understandably anxious about seeing their personal histories in print. It has taken greater courage on their part than persuasion on mine to bring their stories to birth. For them, the process has been painful and therapeutic at the same time.

The fruit of many personal conversations, these vignettes of human struggle and joy are offered as a contribution to the current theological debate. The collection emerges from academic research I undertook into male homosexuality and the priesthood, a subject I have frequently reported on as a religious affairs broadcaster over the past decade. I am based in England but, developing my field of study for this book, I originally set out to profile gay men leading spiritual lives on both sides of the Atlantic. This would enable me to present contrasting male perspectives from Britain and the United States. However, as events unfolded in the Anglican Communion, I extended the scope of my enquiry to include voices from Africa and a number of lesbian Christians who broaden the picture through their own distinctive insights. But, first, the stories need to be set briefly in context.

The Anglican Communion

During 2005, the issue of homosexuality continued to have major ecclesiastical implications with a further rupturing of the Anglican Communion. Although relationships between liberals and evangelicals had been strained over their moral outlooks, the event which precipitated the current conflict was the election in the summer of 2003 of Canon V. Gene Robinson as Diocesan Bishop of New Hampshire. He had all the pastoral, spiritual, and leadership qualities the diocese needed—but he was also living openly and unashamedly with his long-term male partner. Some Anglican primates were not slow in warning that his consecration would cause irreparable damage to the Communion because the practice of homosexuality was still regarded by many as a serious sin. But a few months later, in the face of death threats, the ceremony went ahead. Reports at the time drew attention to the fact that Robinson and his partner, Mark Andrew, felt compelled to wear bullet-proof vests under their garments.

In the days and weeks that followed, the ecclesiastical waters became ever more turbulent as conservative and liberal bishops nailed their colors to the mast. Individual provinces took up opposing positions. The American Anglican Council called the consecration "a grievous day in the history of our Church" and many began to wonder if the Anglican Communion could survive intact. African church leaders were among those who immediately distanced themselves from the consecration. They deplored the actions of those bishops who had taken part, believing them to have already divided the communion and to have violated a holy obligation to guard its faith and unity. Uganda immediately severed its ties with the Episcopal Church.

A statement issued by Archbishop Peter Akinola of Nigeria, on behalf of "Primates of the Global South," said the consecration had clearly demonstrated that authorities within the Episcopal Church considered that "their cultural-based agenda is of far greater importance than obedience to the Word of God, the integrity of the one mission of God in which we all share, the spiritual welfare and unity of the worldwide Anglican Communion, our ecumenical and inter-faith relationships."

Archbishop Benjamin Nzimbi of Kenya went further. He announced that his church would have nothing to do with Bishop Robinson or any of the bishops who had participated. He refused to look upon them as fellow Anglicans. The Kenyans would not accept any support from the Episcopal Church, including missionaries. "We cannot be in the same communion with Robinson, his diocese and the bishops who were in the consecration," he insisted. "The devil has clearly entered the church. God cannot be mocked."

In the ensuing weeks thirteen provinces of the developing world declared themselves out of communion with the American church. The Ugandan church withdrew invitations to representatives of the Episcopal Church to the enthronement of its new archbishop and instead approached a delegation from the American Anglican Council. In a statement of their own, the bishops of the Congo fiercely condemned the churches of the United States and Canada: "In its position of moral keeper, the Church must do all in its power to prevent immorality and itself avoid being corrupted and in turn corrupting the whole world." The emerging divisions were described by the Archbishop of Canterbury, Dr. Rowan Williams, as "a matter of deep regret." He said they would be all too visible in the fact that it would not be possible for Gene Robinson's ministry as a bishop to be accepted in every province in the communion. It was clear, however, that those who had consecrated Gene Robinson had acted "in good faith on their understanding of what the constitution of the American church permits." But the effects on the ministry and witness of the overwhelming majority of Anglicans, particularly in the non-western world, had to be confronted with honesty. "The autonomy of Anglican provinces is an important principle," he went on. "But precisely because we rely on relations more than rules, consultation and interdependence are essential for our health."

However, as Stephen Bates notes in his book *A Church at War*, the Africans and others "did not start refusing aid from the devil-possessed U.S. church." No American missionaries were dismissed. The Council of Anglican Provinces in Africa, chaired by Archbishop Akinola, not only accepted $80,000 for its new headquarters building, but also sent a representative to Washington DC's diocesan convention in early 2004. The diocese of Honduras, whose bishop, Lloyd Bishop, had called on Americans to financially starve the church in the United States, happily accepted renewed aid for a further three years from the Washington diocese, one of the most liberal in the Episcopal Church.[1]

Months earlier, as evangelical power had been tightening its grip on the Church of England, a distinguished theologian at London's Southwark Cathedral, Canon Jeffrey John, had been forced to withdraw as Bishop of Reading before he had even reached for his mitre. He happened to be a celibate homosexual whose same-sex friendship was defined in terms of "companionship and sexual abstinence." The Dean of Southwark, the Very Reverend Colin Slee, said John had become "the victim of appalling prejudice and abuse" which had its main proponents within the Church of England and about whom the church at large "should be deeply penitent." The church had to address the manner in which a relatively small group had sought to undermine the authority of the archbishop and thereby the church as a whole.

"The withdrawal of Canon John's nomination will not only hurt those who are gay," said Colin Slee. "This news will hurt thousands of Christian people who are not gay but believe strongly in God's love and redemption for all his children equally. It is irrelevant to God's love whether people are male or female, slave or free, black or white, gay or heterosexual. We are addressing spiritual apartheid."

Slee thought Jeffrey John had been subjected to a campaign of persecution, not by the press, but by a minority of Christians in England who had exploited the press's natural interest to further their own agenda. They had also used the cultural gulf that existed between a number of developing countries and western churches "to call in reinforcements to blackmail the Anglican Communion with threats of schism because they know they do not actually have a clear mandate beyond their narrow congregations in this country." According to Colin Slee, they made a noise out of all proportion to their size, used monetary wealth as a tool, and were being allowed to set the agenda "in a manner which is deleterious to the church at large."

Then in April 2004, it was suddenly announced that Jeffrey John was to become the new Dean of St. Albans—one level down from a bishopric but an enviable preferment within the Church of England, with responsibility for one of its oldest and finest cathedrals. The appointment had the effect of silencing the hectoring evangelicals who, for once, seemed lost for words. They had maintained that John had been unsuitable for a bishopric because of the need to be a focus of unity. But they had not declared that it was inappropriate for him to be in holy orders, so they could not complain about a change of position, however much of a "plum job" it was. John, who also became rector of the cathedral and abbey church of St. Albans, said at the initial press conference that he was honored. "The Cathedral is a wonderful and holy place. I will be proud to be part of it and hope I can further its work and witness." He also pointed out that, while he would not defy church policy, he would support the state and the church in offering gay people a framework to live their lives within a covenant of faithfulness to each other, regardless of whether it was called "marriage" or not. But he accepted that the word *marriage* in that context was a "red rag to many bulls."

Elsewhere, controversies continued to rage over a decision by the Diocese of New Westminster, Canada, to approve the blessing of gay relationships against the mind of the Anglican Communion, including eleven of its own parishes. Then the Diocese of Toronto announced that it, too, would be embarking on a year-long discussion process on same-gender sanctifications. And so it went on. At its General Convention in the United States, the Episcopal Church passed a resolution saying that all dioceses could develop rites for same-sex blessings based on "the local option" of their bishop. A number wasted little time in setting the wheels in motion. The resolution acknowledged that blessings were already happening in all but three dioceses. The conservatives were reeling.

With a matter of urgency, the Archbishop of Canterbury set up the Lambeth Commission on Communion, chaired by the Archbishop of Armagh, Dr. Robin Eames, to spell out the legal and theological implications of Gene Robinson's consecration. Its nineteen members, drawn from a geographical and theological spectrum, were also asked to discuss the wider implications of the authorization of same-sex blessings by the New Westminster diocese. The commission's views were made public in the Windsor Report, published in the autumn of 2004. It recommended that the provinces of the Anglican Communion should sign up to an Anglican Covenant and adopt a basic "common law." Furthermore, church leaders whose actions had caused the current divisions in the Communion should say they regretted the breach and should consider withdrawing from "representative functions" in the Communion. The commission added that the Archbishop of Canterbury should "exercise very considerable caution" in inviting or admitting the Bishop of New Hampshire "to the councils of the Communion."

Dr. Eames insisted that the unanimous report was not a fudge. It gave very precise details in addressing the issues in the provinces of the Communion. "I like to think that we are learning the realities in a pluralist, sad, and divided world of what it means to understand each other; and I hope that is the sub-text of my report," he commented. The experience of thirty years of violence in Northern Ireland had taught him that reconciliation could not be imposed. It came when people wanted it. Dr. Eames added that, if the report were taken up by the Communion, "reconciliation can become a reality, and not at the cost of truth."

The Commission said that the Episcopal Church should be invited to "regret that the proper constraints of the bonds of affection" were breached in the events that led to his consecration. This would imply that it still wanted to be part of the Anglican Communion. Those who had taken part in Bishop Robinson's consecration should be asked to consider "in all conscience whether they should withdraw themselves from representative functions in the Anglican Communion." This meant those in positions representing the whole of the Communion, such as the Presiding Bishop of the Episcopal Church, Frank Griswold, who had already stepped down as co-chairman of ARCIC, the Anglican-Roman Catholic International Commission.

The Episcopal Church had "breached the bounds of the Communion" by electing and consecrating as bishop a person who, it already knew, had been declared unacceptable to the Anglican Communion. Representations had been made to the commission that this was part of the legitimate diversity of life in the Anglican Communion. But many of the Primates had rejected this, believing it was "not appropriate" to regard this as an example of waiting for a development to be "received" by the Communion. The matter of discipline was "problematic" as there was no central way of imposing it. Nonetheless, Dr. Eames also criticized those primates who had interfered in dioceses beyond their jurisdiction and had offered alternative episcopal oversight to parishes who were troubled by the Episcopal Church's stance. Theirs were equally actions that threatened the common life of the Communion. "Anglican Churches have become a truly international form of Christianity. Our future lies together. We received many submissions and most stressed this desire. Practically speaking, all 44 Anglican Churches have legitimate autonomy to organize their own affairs; yet they are not free to depart unilaterally."

Dr. Eames was supported by the Most Rev. Drexel Gomez, Primate of the West Indies, who emphasized that it had reached the highest degree of consensus. His hope was that "the spirit of Christian charity will transcend the unfortunate styles both sides have of presenting the issues. It is all too easy to give in to demonizing others. I plead for the creation of an environment for the Communion to receive the report without prejudice."

Commenting on the report, Bishop Robinson said gays and lesbians would continue to be "second-class members" of the Anglican Communion so long as it attempted to prevent the consecration of other gay bishops and the blessings of same-sex couples. Meanwhile, Bishop Griswold pointed out that, as Anglicans, they interpreted and lived the gospel in multiple contexts. The differing circumstances of their lives could lead to widely divergent understandings and points of view. His first reading indicated that the report had in mind the containment of differences in the service of reconciliation. But he went on:

Unless we go beyond containment and move to some deeper place of acknowledging and making room for the differences that will doubtless continue to be present in our Communion, we will do disservice to our mission. A life of communion is not for the benefit of the church but for the sake of the world. All of us, regardless of our several points of view, must accept the invitation to consider more deeply what it means to live a life of communion, grounded in the knowledge that "in Christ God was reconciling the world to himself."

Given the emphasis of the report on difficulties presented by our differing understandings of homosexuality, as Presiding Bishop I am obliged to affirm the presence and positive contribution of gay and lesbian persons to every aspect of the life of our church and in all orders of ministry. Other provinces are also blessed by the lives and ministry of homosexual persons. I regret that there are places within our Communion where it is unsafe for them to speak out of the truth of who they are.

The report will be received and interpreted within the provinces of the Communion in different ways, depending on our understanding of the nature and appropriate expression of sexuality. It is important to note here that in the Episcopal Church we are seeking to live the gospel in a society where homosexuality is openly discussed and increasingly acknowledged in all areas of our public life. For at least the last 30 years our church has been listening to the experience and reflecting upon the witness of homosexual persons in our congregations. There are those among us who perceive the fruit of the Spirit deeply present in the lives of gay and lesbian Christians, both within the church and in their relationships. However, other equally faithful persons among us regard same gender relationships as contrary to scripture. Consequently, we continue to struggle with questions regarding sexuality.

The report called the Anglican Communion to reconciliation, which did not mean the reduction of differences to one single viewpoint. In fact, it was the bishop's experience that the fundamental reality of the Episcopal Church was the diverse center, in which a common commitment to Jesus Christ and a sense of mission in his name to a broken and hurting world overrode varying opinions on any number of issues, including homosexuality. That diverse center was characterized by a spirit of mutual respect and affection rather than hostility and suspicion. He hoped some of the ways in which Anglicans had learned to recognize Christ in one another, in spite of strongly held divergent opinions, could be of use in other parts of the Communion.

Bishop John Bryson Chane of Washington was among those who had consecrated Robinson as Bishop of New Hampshire and whose diocese had developed a rite for blessing same-sex unions. He expressed his sadness that the actions they had undertaken in good conscience, bringing hope to one alienated and marginalized population, had themselves engendered alienation and made others feel marginalized. This had not been their intent. "We lament this result and I commit myself to participating fully and energetically in the process of reconciliation through dialog and discernment which is outlined in the Commission's report," he said.

But there were strong words from the Peter Akinola, primate of All Nigeria and Chairman of the Council of Anglican Provinces in Africa, who said the report had correctly noted that the Episcopal Church and the Diocese of New Westminster had pushed the Anglican Communion to the breaking point. It "rightly stated" that they did not listen to the clear voices of the Communion and rejected the counsel of all four Instruments of Unity. It was therefore surprising that the primary recommendation of the report was "greater sensitivity" instead of heartfelt repentance. Already Bishop Griswold had stated that he saw no need to halt welcoming practicing homosexuals into all orders of ministry. In addition, the bishop of New Westminster had indicated that same-sex blessing would continue. "Thus they are hell bent on destroying the fabric of our common life and we are told to sit and wait," Bishop Akinola remarked. He continued:

We have been asked to express regret for our actions and "affirm our desire to remain in the Communion." How patronizing! We will not be intimidated. In the absence of any signs of repentance and reform from those who have torn the fabric of our Communion and, while there is continuing oppression of those who uphold the Faith, we cannot forsake our duty to provide care and protection for those who cry out for our help.

The Bible says that two cannot walk together unless they are agreed. The report rightly observes that if the "call to halt" is ignored "then we shall have to begin to learn to walk apart." The Episcopal Church and Diocese of New Westminster are already walking alone on this and, if they do not repent and return to the fold, they will find that they are all alone. They will have broken the Anglican Communion.

But the Most Rev. Bernard Malango, Primate of Central Africa and a member of the Lambeth Commission, believed the report represented "a genuine way forward for the future of the Anglican Communion." It offered "our brothers and sisters in Christ" very real ways in which they could begin to strengthen their common life in the Lord and to strengthen the workings of the Instruments of Unity so that they would be able to function more effectively in drawing the forty-four churches into greater interdependence and mutual life.

"For me, the very last paragraph of the report is important," he said. "It clearly sets out the fact that as a commission we have aimed to work for healing and restoration, but it also recognizes that there remains the danger that our brothers and sisters may still choose to walk apart. If the recommendations of our report are not taken seriously, then the question of our future together in the Anglican Communion will remain, and greater division may result."

The White House

In the secular world, meanwhile, the momentum toward the legalizing of gay partnerships was growing. The British Government, for example, proposed that same-sex couples, who were prepared to covenant with each other to the same degree of commitment as married partners, should, as far as possible, enjoy identical rights and responsibilities. In the United States, however, certain legislators in the House of Representatives proposed a ban on "gay marriages" to counter state laws granting legal recognition to homosexual unions. President George W. Bush said he wanted to "codify" marriage to ensure it remained "between man and woman."

Vermont's high court allowed its state legislature to ban same-sex marriage as long as it provided an alternative for gays and lesbians called "civil unions," while the Massachusetts Supreme Judicial Court ordered its state legislature to provide nothing less than marriage. After four of the seven justices of the Massachusetts

Supreme Judicial Court had cleared the last obstacle, Massachusetts took the lead among states as the only one to grant the right of civil marriage to same-sex couples. Four other states had created alternative statuses—more or less like marriage. New Jersey enacted a domestic partnership law that provided formal recognition of same-sex relationships, but fell a long way short of marriage. Since the Massachusetts ruling, thirty-seven states have introduced legislation aimed at preserving the traditional definition of marriage as a union between a man and a woman.

Then, in July 2004, efforts failed in the Senate to pass a constitutional amendment that would have effectively outlawed same-sex marriage. The proposed Federal Marriage Amendment, championed by President Bush, was killed for the session after a procedural vote to move the measure to the Senate floor for final consideration failed 48–50. This was 12 votes short of the 60 required by Senate rules. Six Republicans joined 43 Democrats and one independent to defeat the measure. Three Democrats and 45 Republicans voted for it.

The White House released a statement from President Bush in which he was "disappointed" that the amendment was "temporarily blocked" in the Senate and urged the House to take up the matter. "Activist judges and local officials in some parts of the country are not letting up in their efforts to redefine marriage for the rest of America, and neither should defenders of traditional marriage flag in their efforts," he said.

Opponents denounced the failed effort as a political tool during a presidential election year. The president of the Human Rights Campaign, Cheryl Jacques, said that President Bush and the Republican leadership had attempted "to divide America and it backfired, instead dividing their own party. We saw the politics of distraction fail and fail handily."

Were it eventually to get through, the proposed amendment would have the effect of invalidating all state and local domestic partnership laws as well as nullifying civil rights protections based on marital status. It would require a two-thirds majority of both houses of Congress to pass and would then need the approval of three-fourths of the state legislatures to be ratified. Urging people to oppose "writing intolerance" into the United States Constitution, the American Civil Liberties Union commented: "Gay Americans serve in the military, keep our communities safe as firefighters and police officers, staff our hospitals, build our cities, and pay taxes. Denying gay couples the right to marry takes away legal rights in pensions, health insurance, hospital visitations and inheritance that other committed couples enjoy."

Six months after gay and lesbian couples began legally marrying in Massachusetts, opponents of same-sex marriage swept Election Day in November 2004, with voters in eleven states approving amendments to their states' constitutions codifying marriage as an exclusively heterosexual institution. The amendments won in Arkansas, Georgia, Kentucky, Michigan, Mississippi, Montana, North Dakota, Oklahoma, Ohio, Utah, and even Oregon—the one state where gay rights activists had hoped to prevail.

The amendments passed with a 3-to-1 margin in Kentucky, Georgia, and Arkansas, 3-to-2 in Ohio, and 6-to-1 in Mississippi. Bans passed by narrower margins in Oregon, about 57 percent, and Michigan, about 59 percent. Gay rights activists filed challenges to the new amendments in Georgia and Oklahoma.

In Louisiana, a judge struck down a constitutional same-sex marriage ban, approved two months before, on grounds that it improperly dealt with more than one issue by banning not only same-sex marriage but also any legal recognition of domestic partnerships or civil unions. Louisiana's constitution requires that amendments be limited to a single subject.

Three other states that also have single-subject requirements—Georgia, Ohio, and Oklahoma—may face legal challenges similar to the one in Louisiana. The amendments in Mississippi, Montana, and Oregon refer only to marriage, specifying that it should be limited to unions of one man and one woman. The measures in Arkansas, Georgia, Kentucky, Michigan, North Dakota, Ohio, Oklahoma, and Utah call for a ban on civil unions and other partnership benefits as well.

None of these states allowed gay marriage before, but the stakes were highest in Oregon, where city officials in Portland had married nearly 3,000 same-sex couples in spring 2004 before a judge halted the practice. National and local gay rights groups campaigned vigorously in Oregon, raising and spending millions of dollars, but they failed to defeat the amendment.

All of this serves to confirm just how divisive the issue of gay marriage is in certain parts of the U.S. population and clearly sends a signal to anyone thinking about running for public office. Indeed, in the immediate aftermath of the election, many people were surprised when "moral values" appeared to beat terrorism, the economy, and Iraq as the voters' key concern. George W. Bush reversed Al Gore's 2000 win among Roman Catholic voters, securing 52 percent of that vote. The president gained 9 percent among African American Protestant voters and got 78 percent among white evangelicals. All these groups appeared to be concerned about a set of issues bearing on sexuality and relationships, such as abortion, embryonic stem cells, and gay marriage. Evangelical Christians had long warned that they thought the nation's moral values were on the wrong track.

One commentator suggested that, on the matter of gay marriage, the bold actions of San Francisco's mayor, who opened the City Hall for gay weddings in February 2004, simply ran ahead of where many people actually were. This might have played into the hands of the Republicans and become their secret weapon of the campaign. The resulting furor was undoubtedly a factor in the anti-gay marriage bills passed in eleven states:

> In the end, both Bush and Kerry stated their support for "civil unions" but opposed gay marriage. That is actually quite a move. Although it is a mistake, in my view, to blame gays or gay marriage as the source of problems for marriage in our society, it is not a mistake to note that many people feel a deep concern about our high rate of divorce, about single-parent and fatherless families, and the consequences of all this in the lives of children and communities. Unfortunately, and unfairly, this disquiet glommed onto the gay-marriage issue.
>
> Here's the key word on all this: vulnerability. Although the more liberal and often more affluent part of American society focuses on big issues of public policy, tax policy, environmentalism and the war in Iraq, many working-class Americans— once the core Democratic constituency—feel vulnerable on

matters closer to home: family stability and integrity, marriage, children and fatherhood, pornography and cultural permissiveness. My hunch is that many working-class Americans, for whom Bush's paired "family and faith" resonate, perceive liberals and the Democratic Party to be clueless and indifferent to their concerns.[2]

San Francisco resident Patrick Mulcahey, a profile of whom appears in this book, told me that people had speculated on whether Mayor Newsom had lost the election for the Democrats by pressing the gay marriage issue a year too soon. They felt that, without giving the Republicans the threat of same-sex marriage with which to frighten the evangelicals, Americans would have been voting on Bush's "less-than-sterling record" on its own merits, so a Democrat would have replaced him in the White House. Mulcahey, a Roman Catholic, commented: "It would surely give St. Francis, our city's patron saint, a turn to hear us arguing about whether there's a wrong time to do the right thing. I think the marriage question sprang itself on us, the way heart needs will do, before thinking had a chance to catch up. Sometimes I wonder if what we're looking at is the biggest purely semantic furor in history. What is 'marriage'? A union between two men or two women will always differ from a union between a man and a woman who are biologically capable of having children together. Call it whatever you want, make whatever laws you want, that's not going to change. I am not so sure, philosophically, that a union between two men or two women differs so much from the marriage of my late great-aunt Jane, who didn't wed till she was in her seventies. But she and her octogenarian husband were not denied the sacrament, and the lovely bond they formed so late in life was still called marriage. Should it have been called a civil union? That would have broken her heart."

The Vatican

In its own strongly worded document, the Vatican urged Catholic politicians to campaign actively against such liaisons which, it said, were evil and deviant, posing a grave threat to society. Catholic lawmakers were warned that any support of same-sex unions would be "gravely immoral."[3] There was a moral duty on them to oppose such moves publicly.

"There are absolutely no grounds for considering homosexual unions to be in any way similar or even remotely analogous to God's plan for marriage and family," the document said. "Marriage is holy, while homosexual acts go against the natural moral law. Legal recognition of homosexual unions or placing them on the same level as marriage would mean not only the approval of deviant behavior . . . but would also obscure basic values which belong to the common inheritance of humanity."[4]

The guidelines, issued by the Congregation for the Doctrine of the Faith, reiterated church teaching that the homosexual inclination was "objectively disordered" and that homosexual practices were "sins gravely contrary to chastity." They pointed out that people extending cohabitation rights needed "to be reminded that the approval or legalization of evil is something far different from the toleration of evil." Adoptions by gay couples were denounced as "doing violence to these children in the sense that their condition of dependency would be used to place them in an environment that is not conducive to their full human development."[5]

What struck many observers, gay and straight alike, was the political and legislative pressure the Vatican was exerting. As one of them told me, "The Roman Catholic Church doesn't believe in birth control either but nobody hears the Vatican demanding that condoms and birth control pills be outlawed, only that Catholics should not use them."

The Vatican's approach toward matters of sexuality and its embarrassment over the number of cases of sexual abuse among its own clergy have spawned confused thinking, such as the erroneous association of homosexuality with pedophilia. This is clearly irresponsible and damaging, but as the American religious writer David Gibson explains:

> The abuse [in the United States] was largely the result of the actions of emotionally immature homosexual men who preyed on teenage boys. This is dangerous terrain, because it plays into homosexual stereotypes and into the homophobia that lurks

just under the surface of American society and traditional religions. True to form, many Catholics, particularly conservatives, have attacked the presence of homosexuals in the priesthood as the source of the scandal, and by extension, the root of the crisis in Catholicism. . . .

In truth, gay priests did not cause the scandal, nor is the "gaying" of the priesthood over recent decades—a trend that had been widely ignored until the scandal—a cause of the Catholic crisis. Rather, it is a symptom of many other changes in the priesthood. And yet it is a transformation that cannot be brushed aside as irrelevant. The scandal brought the issue of homosexual priests front and center. How the church deals with their presence in the clergy may determine the very future of the priesthood itself, and the daily practice of Catholicism as it has been understood for centuries. The truth is that if homosexuals are banished from the priesthood, that will do nothing to stop sexual abuse and it will do everything to undermine the Catholic Church's understanding of itself as a place where saints are made.[6]

According to Gibson, the number of gay men in the priesthood is rising, even as new priests declare themselves to be more traditional. This points to "a fatal contradiction" in the argument of conservatives who want to "solve" the problem by banishing homosexuals from the priesthood. He discloses that, in America,

many seminaries currently ask candidates about their sexual orientation with the goal of keeping homosexuals out, and yet homosexuals still manage to become priests. More intrusive inquiries would only drive gay men further into the closet of repression and deception, making the priesthood even more of an incubator for unhealthy homosexual activity. The idea of barring gays leads conservatives into an additional bind, because that practice would require a greater reliance on psychological testing, which they have frequently criticized as an imprecise tool for evaluating seminary applicants.[7]

In 2002 the Congregation for Divine Worship and the Discipline of the Sacraments (following consultation with the Congregation for the Doctrine of the Faith) issued a statement clarifying the Vatican's position on whether or not "men with homosexual tendencies" should be ordained. It followed a query to the Congregation for Clergy from a bishop who asked if the practice was "licit." The response was unequivocal:

> Ordination to the diaconate and the priesthood of homosexual men or men with homosexual tendencies is absolutely inadvisable and imprudent and, from the pastoral point of view, very risky. A homosexual person, or one with a homosexual tendency, is not, therefore, fit to receive the sacrament of Holy Orders.[8]

Although the statement was not a ruling as such, it was sent as a guide to bishops' conferences around the world. It remains influential in decision-making procedures about future members of the priesthood. But many others regard the advice as blatantly homophobic (in both tone and content), clearly contradicting the Vatican's own teaching that homosexual people should be treated with respect and not discriminated against.

In general, each candidate for the priesthood is assessed on an individual basis but a firm commitment to celibacy is always required, whatever his sexual orientation. However, in view of what many perceive to be the church's "irrational fear" of homosexuality, those candidates who happen to be gay know it is wise to keep their heads down. In the current climate, they could be regarded (however improperly) as potential "problems." There is no denying that spiritual leaders are on a state of high alert and, in the process, prospective priests, in touch with their sexuality and unashamed of it, are falling victim to the church's anxiety at this time. Understandably at pains to protect the future reputation of the church, bishops, vocations directors, and seminary principals are exercising extreme caution at every turn, as this book shows.

Furthermore, it seems a number of priests who are secretly homosexual are coming to resent the new breed of openly gay candidate intent on living less surreptitiously. Acting out of envy, perhaps, they sometimes report these young men to those in power, even when they have been their friends. Such betrayals may endanger the candidates' chances of going to seminary, let alone being ordained.

Bishops seem keen to show pastoral concern toward gay people prepared to abide by the rules, but one former student claimed the system of selection encouraged them to become "gifted liars" because they would immediately come under suspicion once it was known they were homosexual. "This is precisely the skill of the pedophile—to lie or cover up," he told me.

> The pedophile gets through because his trait is deception. He knows what and what not to say. But the more trusting gay candidate, who has integrity because he is at ease with himself, is often forced into deception because he doesn't want to ruin his chances. The psychological testing should therefore focus more on detecting truthfulness than uncovering sexual orientation.

Even those homosexuals who get through to seminaries aren't necessarily home free. A former seminarian told me that some openly gay students at his college had been asked to leave. Other seminaries are known to have expelled men who confessed to visiting gay nightclubs. All this is somewhat ironic in view of the large number of homosexuals already in the priesthood. Honesty can evidently breed contempt. On the other hand, as an interview for *Disclosures* makes clear, a seminarian who discovers he is gay during training need not necessarily receive harsh treatment. "Tim" speaks of the pastoral and financial support he received after telling his bishop he was leaving college to begin a new life.

The Psycho-Spiritual Dynamic

For some people, the words *gay* and *homosexual* still evoke the same reaction that the term *cancer* once engendered—the unmentionable. But many years have passed since homosexuality was generally regarded as an illness or a pathology. Nonetheless it is still difficult to write about the subject positively without appearing political. It seems that all the public skirmishes over biblical texts, church teaching, and morality obscure the psychological dimension of being gay, which is all too readily overlooked.

An episode of the British television series *Midsomer Murders*, broadcast in 2004, illustrates the point. Set in the publishing world, the episode contained, as its sub-plot, a gay intrigue. Detective Chief Inspector Tom Barnaby (John Nettles) had cause to question retired detective-turned-author Harry Poulson (Michael N. Harbour), who was evidently homosexual.

"Harry, we've known each other now for, what, thirty years?" checks Barnaby, treading carefully. "And for most of that time I have known, well, all of us have known, about your orientation. And I can quite understand why, you know, you felt the need to keep it a secret."

A shocked, sad, and painfully exposed Poulson pauses, then lowers his voice almost hauntingly, "Can you?"

Momentarily tongue-tied, Barnaby concedes, "All right. No I can't."[9]

The scene epitomizes the fear that grips many homosexuals as they weigh up the pros and cons of self-disclosure. As the reaction of Harry Poulson so searchingly suggests, the psychological complexities of gay people are hard to fathom from the outside.

The self hides many secrets. But nowhere are they exposed more dramatically than in *The Talented Mr. Ripley*, that stunning and disturbing film by Anthony Minghella about a young man who chooses to become a fake somebody rather than a real nobody.[10]

Based on the international bestseller by Patricia Highsmith (who was herself lesbian), the elegantly shot movie is set primarily in *la dolce vita* of sun-drenched southern Italy in the late 1950s. It is a lifestyle that Tom Ripley (Matt Damon) craves and Dickie Greenleaf (Jude Law) already possesses: a hedonistic world of coffee-drinking, sunbathing, jazz-playing, and yachting on the blue waters off the Amalfi coast. On his uppers in a depressing New York basement, Ripley has been secretly commissioned by Greenleaf's father to travel to Italy to persuade the son to return home to America. But on arriving in Europe, Ripley is immediately mesmerized by Greenleaf's existence and even further alienated from his own. Moreover, Ripley (a closeted homosexual) seems to be falling in love with Greenleaf himself.

Inebriated, however, by a cocktail of desire, rejection, and inadequacy, Ripley not only kills Greenleaf, but also becomes him. As mystery surrounds the playboy's sudden disappearance, Ripley's natural talent for impersonation leads him into an imbroglio of deceit and subterfuge. As soon as one or two others become suspicious, they too are murdered, including a gay musician who had offered Ripley the best chance of love. But, by then, Ripley is not certain who he really is. He knows he can survive only if he continues his double life. As Minghella comments, "Ripley, always looking for love, always looking to love and be loved, has to kill his opportunity for love . . . in annihilating self, assuming someone's identity, Ripley is condemned never to be free to be truly himself ever again."[11]

Although the homosexual motif is not allowed to dominate, the film offers an unambiguous message about concealing and disguising one's real identity. Like a number of those profiled on the following pages, gay and lesbian people who live in trepidation of their true sexuality becoming known might resonate with elements of Tom Ripley's character. I have watched the film many times and on each occasion am struck by the way Ripley becomes so adept at camouflage and mendacity that he even ends up tricking himself without realizing it. As Minghella observes, "If Ripley is blessed and cursed by one thing, it is his ability to turn on a dime, to reel off the most elaborate and plausible riffs of fantasy."[12]

This is precisely how some gay people are forced to behave. Certain situations can induce irrational but understandable fear in those who do not have the confidence to claim who they really are. Christ may have said that the truth sets people free, but for many homosexuals, including those in the church, the fear of their own self-identity keeps them locked in psychological captivity.

Following the labyrinthine devices of Ripley to pretend to be who he is not, I was reminded of gay men who are married or in partnerships with women (a much larger percentage, it is generally thought, than many people realize); of those who have donned collars and cassocks to hide their sexuality in the priesthood; and of homosexuals who have sadly become habitual liars because they live in the guise of heterosexuality by day and in the secrecy of their own homosexuality by night—it is only in darkness that they can breathe, as such, and then only nervously.

Indeed, some seem so ashamed of their true selves that they become adept at concocting scenarios almost every day, deceiving their families, friends, and colleagues. They might even be in committed relationships, but are so frightened of anybody knowing that they become seasoned practitioners in the art of ruse. In the heterosexual world, there is no such pressure to deceive, unless one partner happens to be having an affair. Some gay people are, however, so psychologically trapped that although they might be in the most loyal of relationships they *act as though* they were involved in an illicit liaison.

Two male friends, for example, might share a house in an almost exclusively heterosexual neighborhood. Regardless of whether they are lovers, the families who live around them will probably assume they are gay. Those same residents might occasionally gather in the street to gossip about a reality on their own doorsteps. The men don't look queer. In fact, they actually appear quite "ordinary," even pleasant. But their proximity can be unnerving. Less assured gay men might still feel obliged to *act as though* they are heterosexual because a suspicious stare or an ambiguous gesture hurts them so much. "This is my new roommate, Robin. He's got a new job in the area and is looking for somewhere to live. His family is still in the city." Or, "I'd like you to meet Craig. He's often here weekends because his girlfriend has to work."

None of this is healthy living, of course, and yet, for some gays and lesbians, deception has become a natural component in a psychological survival kit for a homophobic world. But the consequences can be disastrous in terms of personal integrity and self-worth. Words spoken hesitatingly by Ripley to Peter Smith-Kingsley (Jack Davenport) in the final scene of *The Talented Mr. Ripley* perhaps spell a warning for homosexuals unable to own who they are: "I know. I'm lost, too. I'm going to be stuck in the basement, aren't I, that's my, that's my—terrible and alone and dark—and I've lied about who I am, and where I am, and so nobody can ever find me."[13]

More than thirty years ago, in the language of his time, the Dutch psychiatrist W. G. Sengers pointed out that "the great suffering of the homosexual" was brought about chiefly by a deep-seated resistance to own his emotions. He believed a homosexual could become "available to himself" only if he were able to overcome this self-imposed hurdle and stop allowing the prejudices of others to determine how he felt about himself.

Erotic feelings toward a person of the same sex can be experienced only as positive, says Sengers. Love is beautiful, enjoyable, pleasant, and liberating. The strong attraction between two people of the same sex should be considered nothing other than valuable and enriching. But in reality this is not always the case. The growing awareness of such emotions often creates a sense of shame, low self-esteem, and the fear of being considered "abnormal." Feelings of love and attraction that are in themselves positive, argues Sengers, are condemned by the very people who experience them. "The pressure leading to condemnation must be strong," Sengers writes. "What is good must be called bad, what is positive must become negative. It amounts to adapting his own feelings to what others say about them."[14] When a gay man finds himself in that situation, it is extremely difficult to make his intimate feelings of love and attraction his own. But in denying them, he constructs a strong wall of resistance that is hard to penetrate or break through. It is not the homosexual feelings themselves, but the resistance against them, that often constitutes the burden that gay people shoulder.

According to Sengers, there are two main levels of resistance. The first is when homosexual inclinations are completely denied, not only to others, but primarily by the gay person himself. This cuts himself off from his most personal, intimate, and creative feelings. He becomes rigid, impersonal, and distant, while giving the impression that he has everything under control. This form of denial causes great harm to the personality, says Sengers, and results in emotional poverty. The second level of resistance emerges in contexts where the homosexual understands his feelings but is tortured by the fear that anyone else should detect them. As a result, he experiences social isolation, even when he is in the company of others. He uses up energy in constantly pretending he is "normal." He never feels relaxed enough to express his true feelings. This can lead to obsessive tendencies. He becomes so preoccupied with the fear of being recognized as gay that his sexual feelings are constantly in his mind, haunting him day and night. They force him to sexualize his total existence. Every situation becomes filled with danger as he remains in a constant state of vigilance to prevent anyone from discovering the truth. His sexual life, therefore, stands little chance of forming a unity with the rest of his personality.

Sengers's point is that only when gay people become available to themselves can they relate meaningfully to their emotions and form natural relationships with others. Feelings—whether homosexual or heterosexual in origin, whatever the individual's orientation—touch the core of one's inner life. If these powerful emotions are sealed off or disguised, they can cause psychological, and, one might add, spiritual, damage, as borne out by some accounts in this book.

Discussions in the church have tended to center on whether a homosexual is "practicing" or not, a distinction rarely drawn in the heterosexual world. Although such differentiation has become common currency, there are those who feel it ultimately devalues the debate, serving only to undermine the gift of wholeness to which sexuality points. As the Roman Catholic theologian Daniel Helminiak has argued, sexuality goes straight to the essence of a person and means much more than any physical expression:

> Attached to a person's sexuality is the capacity to feel affection, to delight in someone else, to get emotionally close to another person, to be passionately committed to him or her. Sexuality is at the core of that marvellous human experience, being in love—to be struck by the beauty of another and be drawn out of yourself, to become attached to another human being so powerfully that you easily begin measuring your life in terms of what's good for someone else as well as for yourself.[15]

At the heart of any journey toward such wholeness is a divine call to love vulnerably. It is a vocation for all Christian people but, perhaps, especially so for gay men and women who have a special understanding of vulnerability through their own search for love and belonging. The Catholic theologian James Alison makes a similar point in one of the interviews.

The word *vulnerability* comes from the Latin, *vulnus*, a wound. To be vulnerable is to be capable of being physically or emotionally hurt. It is to be exposed to danger or criticism. It is to be accessible, assailable, defenseless, expugnable, liminal, open to attack, precarious, sensitive, susceptible, tender, thin-skinned, unprotected, and wide open. Vulnerability is about non-immunity, insecurity, nakedness. Loving vulnerably is the purpose of God himself. It involves a willingness to put oneself at risk. To suffer. Love and suffering are of a piece.

According to another Catholic writer, Richard Woods, the meaning of homosexual experience is

> the creativity of suffering made possible by deep love—and by that love, overcoming suffering, not avoiding it. Suffering must be gone *through*—not around. Resurrection means that on the other side of suffering willingly undergone as a sign of our solidarity with all men and women is the reality of a greater joy and peace . . . The great power of the gay person and the gay community lies in the potential to love—to love beyond the surface tension of immediate gratification, and to love despite suffering and rejection at the hands of the persons whose lives are immeasurably enriched by the fact there *are* gay persons around to love them and to suffer for them.[16]

Much has been written about the wound and gift of homosexuality. In the English language, the word *wound* and the word *blessing* have the same root, while in French *les blesses* translates as "the wounded." As one contemplative has written, "Our wounds are ultimately our greatest source of blessing because they become one with the wounds of our humble God."[17] So perhaps the wound of homosexuality is, after all, a blessing for the church. I remember an English Catholic priest once suggesting to me that "gay people are an underground stream nourishing the institution, often from the hidden corners of the earth."

The Australian author Maurice Shinnick, himself a Catholic priest, has gone as far as to define homosexuality as a "remarkable gift" because against all the odds—in the face of civil penalties, medical labels of illness, and church classification of sin—gay men and lesbian women have emerged from an age of dark ignorance to recognize and honor their own dignity and worth. They are, he maintains, "part of the church, part of the Body of Christ, a gift to the community—bringing particular qualities and insights, not in spite of, but because of, their gayness."[18]

With equal vigor, the Episcopal theologians L. William Countryman and M. R. Ritley have suggested that gay and lesbian Christians are "gifted by otherness." Rather than trying to justify their existence to the majority heterosexual community within the church, they should not shirk from speaking from their own experiences. The stories of lesbian and gay Christians constitute "the enriching of the community's fabric."[19]

It is in such a spirit that this book has been compiled. Each profile, based on a conversation, is a reflection in its own right. The choice of subjects owes as much to the art of serendipity as it does to friendships and journalistic contacts, resulting in a remarkable range of experiences: from a poet who grew up in Nigeria, believing he was an abomination, to a writer with his own tale of freedom in California; from two priests living secretly as a lesbian couple in the United Kingdom to a lesbian couple living openly as priests and partners in the United States; and from a South African artist who once drank poison when he realized he was homosexual to a former schoolmaster in Northern Ireland who thinks gay and lesbian people are teaching a divided province a lesson or two in overcoming religious prejudice. Where anonymity was requested, a new given name has been used in order to honor the right of privacy. People's ages and personal circumstances remain as they were at the time of the original interview. The contributors speak, of course, entirely from their own perspectives but hope others will learn from their experiences. I owe each of them a debt of deep gratitude for sharing their stories so candidly, and I extend my sincere thanks to Michael Wilt and all the team at Cowley Publications for their dedicated work on the American edition of this book.

The tales are invariably surprising, often moving, and always piercingly honest. The connection between "being gay" and "feeling called" is particularly intriguing and mysterious.

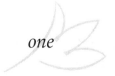

one

Heart and Soul

"My father refused to attend the wedding and my mother came only because my sister threatened to quit speaking to her if she didn't," discloses Sandra as she recalls the joyful day she married her partner, Katie, in Vermont—the first state in the United States to allow the legal joining of same-sex couples. "I'm not sure my father totally realizes that he can never make right what he did in choosing not to come to our wedding. It hurt. It still hurts. But I've come to a place of pity for those who would discard me because of my sexuality."

At the time Sandra and Katie were living in the state capital, Montpelier, where they attended the local Episcopal Church. The rector agreed to bless their union in the church, but the bishop of the diocese did not allow priests to perform the civil union ceremony itself. Neither partner objected because they think the church should not be in the business of creating legal agreements such as civil marriage and civil unions. It ought, they believe, "to be all about blessing the unions—regardless of orientation of the partners—before the community of gathered believers." A member of the parish happened to be a retired Vermont State Supreme Court Justice, and he agreed to take on the civil role. So the day before the church blessing, Sandra and Katie were "joined in civil union" on church property (in the meditation garden) in front of their rector and, ironically, the mother and siblings of Sandra's father. He kept his promise and stayed away.

The next afternoon, supported by all their friends, Sandra and Katie processed down the aisle for their parish's first same-sex blessing. Sandra wrote the liturgy but was precluded by the policy of the diocese from using the words *marriage* or *sacrament*, so she chose *covenant* instead—a more biblically appropriate word anyway, she felt—Sandra invited her former New Testament seminary professor, "who writes the most amazing prayers," to bestow the blessing. "There was lots of wonderful music, we washed one another's feet as a sign of service to one another, and we rejoiced," Sandra told me. "Katie is an artist and designed our wedding rings. They are silver bands, with two separate, but intertwined, endless knots on top. They're simple but significant in describing the way we view our relationship. In order to separate these knots, one must destroy the individual knots—not a desirable choice. We followed the service with ice cream and cake, and went kite-flying at Montpelier's town park, which is on the side of a mountain. It would have been hard for the day to have been more perfect. The only cloud was a note my father sent me a few days before, telling me what a horrible disappointment I was to him and how he'd rather I 'ran naked through Harlem than do this' (which is, in his mind, the worst thing a white woman could ever do)."

Sandra was living in Indiana when Vermont passed the civil union law. She and Katie moved to Vermont for work when the law came into active status, so they watched as the first couples were joined in civil union. Vermont's law is clear in stating that civil union is in effect the same as marriage; it merely uses a different name in terms of legal rights and responsibilities. The couple took advantage of the civil union law because they were living in Vermont so they simply followed the course that most committed couples choose—a legal formalization of the relationship "that (for us at least) included the integral blessing and commitment to accountability that the religious side of such formalization calls for." Sandra and Katie subsequently moved to Massachusetts, where they waited for that state's Supreme Judicial Court to make its decision on the question of marriage rights for same-sex partners, as well as through the six-month stay of their ruling in favor of same-sex marriage to allow the state legislature to respond. When, on May 18, 2004, Massachusetts law changed and recognized the right to same-sex marriage as well as acknowledged Vermont's Civil

Union law as being legal marriage, they suddenly found themselves officially married there as well. "Astonishingly, the heavens did not open up and rain down fire on the Cambridge city hall, nor was there a plague of any sort to be had throughout the state," laughs Sandra. "I guess that, in the final summation, God wasn't that interested in the legal goings on of humanity."

Well-read and a gifted communicator, Sandra is an energetic woman with strong opinions and a deeply held belief in empowerment for the common good. She has a finely tuned sense of humor and is regarded by those who know her as a trustworthy confidant. The view that, somehow, her marriage to Katie adversely affects the marriage of a heterosexual couple they do not even know is, to her way of thinking, bizarre. Sandra's fails to grasp how their marriage can have any tangible effect on anyone else's.

As for those who believe the gay couple is flying in the face of God's will by marrying, Sandra would like to know how they can de-legitimize her process of prayerful discernment so casually. How can the anti-gay folks, she wonders, claim that their understanding of God's will is better than the one she and Katie have understood when they, as a committed partnership, have prayerfully sought God's guidance? It is a false piety and, to some extent, bibliolatry, which infuriates her.

"What makes any of the anti-Gene Robinson camp truly believe that their discernment and prayer are better than Gene's?" Sandra asks. "Gene Robinson has said publicly that he spent tremendous amounts of time in prayer regarding his appointment as a bishop, not to mention his praying about being the first openly—and the key word here is *openly*—gay man to become a bishop. Gene has also said that his discernment has led him to believe that God approves of his becoming a bishop. But the central question is: how can we ever know the mind of God? Since we are never able to know for absolutely sure what God wants for us today, now, in this moment, we must do our best to muddle though. So if we're muddling through, doesn't it make sense that the decisions we make be ones that fall on the side of love? Personally, when I come to stand before the throne of judgment (to sound really evangelical for a moment), I'd much rather have God say to me, 'Sandra, you were too loving' than to have God say to me, 'Sandra, you were right.' I'd rather be wrong and accused of being too loving by the one who created love, than be right. Why is the church so afraid of erring on the side of love? Jesus had no such fear."

At the time of our interview, election fever was gripping the United States and the matter of gay marriage was never far from the political headlines Sandra was monitoring closely. "I liked it when both candidates were asked if they felt being gay was a choice. Bush admitted he didn't know. Now, we all knew he was hedging because he wanted both the anti-gay bigots as well as conservative gay people to vote for him. Of course, he made both groups angry by giving such a non-answer. That said, for him to have admitted not knowing was huge. Kerry was quite firm in his answer to the same question—that being gay was not a choice. I think gays and gay marriage were being used as an ancillary wedge issue so as to avoid talking about the actual issues facing the United States—an intractable war, job loss, general economic slowdown, abominable healthcare access and the like."

Born in Baltimore, Maryland, Sandra has lived in a dozen different states. Sandra and her sister were taken by their parents to church "whenever it was convenient." She semi-jokingly says she was raised "heathen," but senses her mother and father would take exception to that notion. They attended various denominations, such as the United Church of Christ, Dutch Reformed tradition, Reformed Church of America, and the Presbyterian Church USA. Sandra also spent most of her pre-university education in several different Roman Catholic schools "because the public schools in those areas were particularly atrocious." Ethnically, her father's side of the family was Mennonite (Anabaptist), though her paternal grandfather left the church when he married. Some of his siblings remained Mennonite and she knew them well when growing up.

"In my last year of secondary school, I came to believe that God did in fact exist, and that God was not out to get me—that was quite a revelation to me at the time on both counts," Sandra explained. "I began to read the Bible for the first time and discovered that much of what I'd been taught about this collection of books was simply not tenable. I went on to attend a Mennonite Church-owned university through the generosity of a great aunt. During the obligatory Bible classes, I discovered that Anabaptist theology was very much in line with the theology I was forming for myself as I read the Bible on my own. So I became an adherent to Anabaptism (which is a collection of several small Protestant denominations coming out of the Radical Reformation—a group of people who didn't feel Luther's reforms went far enough to reclaim Christianity. Anabaptists are best known for being the historic peace churches in Western Christianity, as well as for what is known as 'adult' or 'believer's' baptism.). I now realize that I should have 'always' known I was not straight. Unfortunately, it took a major event in my thirtieth year to actually sort that out."

In the late 1990s Sandra was working for the Mission Board of the Mennonite Church as their primary writer and photographer. The board seconded her to an organization that worked to build bridges of communication and peace throughout the Middle East. She traveled continuously for more than a year. But then she fell ill and eventually had to return home. During her absence a very close female friend had been living in her house and taking care of her cat—"as dear to me as any child could ever be." When Sandra got back, her health condition deteriorated and there was "a massive falling out" with the woman. A mutual friend, who also happened to be pastor of the church they both attended, suggested that the disagreement was based on Sandra's being "in love" with the woman but being unwilling to admit it. "Silly as it might sound, this was an amazing thought to me. Exhausted as I was, I decided to test the assertion, devoting significant meditation and prayer time to the question for several weeks. In the end, I realized two very important things. First, I was bisexual (meaning I fall pretty much in the middle of the sliding scale of sexuality) and, second, I was not 'in love' or even infatuated romantically with my friend. The first revelation gave me a freedom I'd not known I was missing. The latter gave me the ability to tell the pastor friend just what I thought of her idea and also the leave to let the friendship go and walk away."

The fact that Sandra is bisexual is "actually harder than I think it would be to be lesbian," she suggests. "Both gay and straight people puzzle over the notion of bisexuality. 'Does it mean you have a partner of each gender all of the time?' 'Does it mean you can't commit to just one gender?' 'You just want it both ways, don't you?' 'Oh, you're just a lesbian and haven't come to terms with it yet.' People who are further out on the sliding scale at either end seem mistrustful of bisexuality. For me, it just means that, when I assess someone's attractiveness in a romantic way, gender is not a factor. That's all. I'm a very monogamous sort of person. More than one partner would just confuse me! I remember being quite surprised with my lack of knowledge of myself when I came to that great realization regarding where I happened to fall on the sexuality spectrum. I'd been working for years to deal with some rather ugly childhood traumas and I thought I'd gotten a pretty good handle on the person I was. So to devote concentrated time to exploring my sexuality in the specific and coming to realize that I'd misunderstood myself was somewhat shocking. That said, once it dawned, I was fine with it. The hard parts have been in the reactions of others."

Sandra already held a Master of Divinity degree from a Mennonite seminary which qualified her for pastoral ministry in the Mennonite Church. But were she to enroll in the seminary today, she would not be allowed to receive the degree because gay people are not allowed in active ministry in the Mennonite Church. "When I came to an understanding of my sexuality," she admits, "I was essentially kicked out of my church too. So there has been a lot of conflict along the way in terms of my relationship with the church—but not in terms of my faith. I had begun theologically exploring sexuality issues when I was in university (my minor area of study was the Bible and religion). I came to this believing that gay people were living outside of God's will for humanity. However, as I studied the stories of the Bible and the various opinions of scholars, I reached a new understanding (which, ironically, was at odds with the view of most of my professors). I came to appreciate that the over-arching character of the Bible was that it is largely a series of stories that illustrate our human relationship with God, one that has always been contentious, but has also progressed. If there is any one thing we should unhesitatingly be able to say about

God after reading the Bible, it is that God loves God's creation—all of it. And so if God created humanity and God loves God's creation unconditionally, then it follows that, as viewed on a sliding scale of 'straightness' and 'gayness,' sexuality (like personality and any other number of human traits) is part of what is loved unconditionally by God and therefore gay people are not living outside of God's will."

As the years have passed, Sandra has become more convinced that this is true. God is about communion and community, she asserts. Sexuality cannot be changed any more than the color of one's eyes. "Sure you can purchase colored contact lenses (as you can put on a facade that you're straight), but it doesn't change the actual color of your eyes. So, if sexuality is as innate to one's self as something like eye color, then it cannot be a choice," she argues. "And if it is not a choice, then it becomes about being faithful to the call of God in this world 'doing justice, loving mercy and walking humbly with your God' as the prophet Micah says."

Not long after Sandra had come to understand herself as bisexual, she was hired as the technical director of the theatre program at the university where she had studied for her undergraduate degree. The college is owned by the Mennonite Church. It is not possible, she points out, to be both openly gay *and* employed by the Mennonite Church. When she began dating Katie, Sandra deliberately kept the romance quiet because she knew she could lose her job, even though it is technically illegal to fire someone on the grounds of their sexuality. But one day, she was informed that her contract was not being renewed. "This was normally a routine sort of thing—a contract was always renewed," she explained. "As I had done nothing wrong, I asked why this was happening. They refused to tell me. Some time later, I found out that the pastor had gone to the college administration, told them I was gay and was seeing a woman. They soon got rid of me."

Sandra has even experienced discrimination and rejection much closer to home. For about a decade, she had a special friend for whom she babysat. The friend and her husband regularly told their kids that they hoped they would grow up to be like Sandra. "That was an incredible honor for me," says Sandra. "I loved those kids and they loved me. Moreover, I considered this woman to be a very good friend. We went to breakfast together every other Saturday morning to talk, pray, and just be friends. Then I met someone to whom I was attracted. Katie and I began seeing one another. It was really good. I was falling in love. It was so incredibly amazing for me. I'd never been in love before in my life. I was floating on air. So naturally I decided to share my excitement with my friend. I told her about Katie, how I felt, that we were exploring what it was to be together. The friend was horrified—shocked almost beyond words. In a crowded restaurant, she got up, began telling me how I was sinning, going to hell, needed to repent—and all of that quite loudly. She followed this by proclaiming (boldly enough for the whole restaurant to hear) that she was going to tell the church that I was 'a dirty faggot' and that I was never to come near her children ever again."

A week or so went by without a further word from this "friend." Then, one evening, the woman showed up at Sandra's door with three others from the church who concluded that Sandra was possessed by a demon and needed an exorcism. "And this was not at all like a Southern Baptist/Evangelical sort of congregation," said Sandra, who refused to take part. "They actually tried to force their way into my house. I had to pick up the phone and threaten to dial the police emergency number to get them to leave."

Such rejection from the Mennonite community has been hard to come to terms with. Sandra believes she gave much of her time, energy, and talents to the denomination and made a great many friends, some of whom no longer speak to her. Sandra's writing and photographs even won national awards for the mission board. Yet, because of her sexuality, the church is prohibited from ever hiring her again. "What changed?" she asks herself. "Only a better understanding of myself—and I fell in love with the wrong-gender person. There's a part of me that wants never to look back. But I suppose it hurts as much as it does because I want more for them. I want them to understand. I want to make them accept me and all of the other gay Mennonites. But I know I can't do that. So, instead, I pity the ones who hate me because I love differently than they do, and I cherish those who continue to be dear friends."

One person whom Sandra also considered a friend for some

fifteen years still sends a card for her birthday. But in it the woman always includes a missive about Sandra's damnation and how it is not too late for her to repent and be healed. She no longer responds to these annual dispatches. "I don't understand that kind of hatred. I'm glad I don't. And I do believe it takes a tremendous amount of hatred to so thoroughly reduce me to my sexuality as she has."

Gay people bring no greater or lesser gifts to the church than any other person, Sandra believes. Gayness is simply an element of what goes into making up an individual. To focus on sexuality as distinctive is ridiculous, she feels. There are so many more pressing problems such as extreme global poverty, oppression of women, rampant war, starvation, and preventable disease. "It really and truly makes me furious that the church has its nose in people's beds when there are real crises being completely ignored. But claiming victim status anywhere is another thing that gets my blood to boil. Everyone has, at some point, in some way, been a victim of something. Some victimization is unspeakably horrid. But we must learn to move beyond the bad things that have happened in life. If we give free rein to victimization for any reason, then the ones who do the victimizing have won. The way to keep them from winning is to choose to stand up, learn from what happened, allow it to make you a more diverse, stronger person, and go out into the world better than you were before. When I write that, it makes it sound like I think it's easy. I know firsthand that it's not. But it *is* the only way. It is a choice; a hard, difficult, painful, seemingly impossible choice, but a choice all the same. All things are possible. I have to believe that or I'll stop getting out of bed in the mornings (and I really do enjoy my first cup of tea every day)."

Sandra admits to not being "a big gay pride" or "gay community" sort of person, although she and Katie subscribe to the gay news magazine *The Advocate* to keep abreast of developments in the gay world. "It's not from a self-loathing or anything like that. It's just that neither of us want to be defined by our sexuality, which is only a very small part of who we are. True, it's an important part because it affects so much else, but it's still relatively small. I claim a sense of bemused surprise at those who choose to define much of their self through their sexuality. I make no judgment about it. I simply don't understand. Nonetheless, those who say 'love the sinner; hate the sin' make me livid with anger. No one can be called upon to separate out one's sexuality without grave damage done to the whole person.

"Katie and I just want to be a family with one another and with any kids that may or may not ever come along. We laugh together, cry together, sometimes argue, enjoy the making up, and just live— like any other reasonably healthy couple. There is nothing particularly remarkable about us. Without Katie, though, my life would be less. Our relationship is like God's knitting together two souls into a big, pink fuzzy sweater. Yes, I want there to be legal and church recognition of my relationship with Katie. But the lack of it does not make the relationship go away. What it does do is make our lives more difficult in a myriad of legal ways, as well as drive us out of the church. I'm Celtic enough in my spirituality to know that I don't need to be a member of a group that meets weekly to be a Christian. But the community is important to me, and I miss it when it's not there. Being a minister is a central part of my self-identity, but right now it's too difficult for me to be part of a formalized ministry structure. I love preaching, but there's nowhere for me to do that right now. It's not easy feeling rejected because I love someone that some people don't approve of. But I'll take what I have with Katie over the rest of them every single time.

"The only thing in my life more important than my relationship with Katie is learning to know God; which has always been tempestuous for me. More than once, I've stood at the edge of the sea, shaking my fist at heaven and telling God to bugger off because I don't get my way nearly often enough—ok, well, mostly never. But I take seriously the Shema, the daily Jewish prayer. And I take the call within Micah seriously. I take Jesus' call to social justice in this world's realm quite seriously. I want to do what I'm supposed to do, but it's hard when so many people in the body that claims a corner on the market of knowing God says I'm unacceptable.

"Truth be told, I'm a pretty dismal example of a servant of God. But I do keep trying. I keep seeking, asking, questioning, and praying that my meager attempts at faithfulness will further God's work in this world's realm.

"God's call in my life is difficult. But I hope I can keep on."

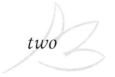

two

Beyond Words

"It's interesting that we're talking about being gay and Catholic," mused Patrick Mulcahey, "because those are the two things I almost never think about—no more than the color of my hair."

Patrick is a former television writer who has won four Emmy awards, including one for his work on the popular American soap *General Hospital*. For nearly two decades, he has been in a relationship with a real-life medic. Dr. Ken Mills is chief of staff at St. Mary's Hospital, San Francisco. "We gave each other rings at some point along the line," Patrick said wryly. "We've taken part in these mass marriage ceremonies for gay couples several times. But if gay people could be married in churches or anywhere else in San Francisco, I don't know whether we would drag ourselves out of our nineteen-year-old relationship and race down to be the first ones there. When the Roman Catholic Church decided that girls could be acolytes, I don't think too many fifty-year-old women rallied to the call. What our commitment is, is not in question. I think it would be in keeping with the traditions of our church that, if it ever did bless same-sex relationships, it would make a distinction between such a ceremony and what it has traditionally considered marriage to be: that is, a sacrament where there is the possibility of children."

Our conversation was taking place at a time when the legalizing of gay marriage was a hotly debated topic in the United States. The twin blasts that had come from President Bush and the Pope had "confounded everything and everybody." In any case, said Patrick, gay marriage was not something the gay community was necessarily

of one mind about. But the arguments against it had been so preju-
dicial and full of holes that it would have been impossible not to
argue against them. The gay community had spoken out vigorously,
sounding as though all its members were pro-gay marriage. Patrick
didn't think that was an issue every lesbian and gay person had reflected on that deeply. And they certainly didn't seem to be making
distinctions between civil unions and religious unions.

As for being a member of the Catholic Church, which coined
words like "disordered" and "evil" when speaking of homosexuality, it was "just so much noise," a stance that invited argumenta-
tion. The mental history of the human race was not a history of its
arguments but a history of ideas. Arguments followed ideas. Could
the Bible be used to support slavery by argument? Certainly,
thought Patrick. Slavery took place for a long time until, one
morning, everyone woke up and thought it preposterous. What
changed? asked Patrick The arguments didn't cease. People simply
began to construct new arguments that moved in the opposite direction. Nowhere in the Beatitudes did Christ say, "Blessed is he
who has the best argument." God was not accessed through arguments, so arguing with edicts from Rome seemed pointless. The language was regrettable but Patrick did not feel particularly insulted.
His faith life was not impeded by the views of a few Vatican officials. The loving kindness that he was drawn to in other Catholics
was not reflected in the language of these papal documents, so he
did not really recognize them or understand where they were
coming from. To him being a Catholic was exactly analogous to
being an American. He had not decided it. He had been born into
it. There was nothing he could have done about it. The church's
teaching on homosexuality was "all fantastically and obviously ordered the wrong way" but beyond his power to fix. But he did have
a choice: he could reject the teachings of the church completely or
not. He had decided neither to reject his citizenship of the United
States—nor his membership of the Catholic Church.

"I'm certainly not important enough to ex-communicate, so nobody really cares particularly what I believe," Patrick went on. "But
the church is going to have to discover that it's painted itself into a
corner about gay people. From time to time they find themselves

obliged to recognize that such an individual as the homosexual person exists. They state that he or she must be counseled to celibacy for their entire life. But the language, intrinsically disordered itself, makes it pretty clear that what they are positing, as far as I can tell, is that God created only homosexual persons defectively. Other persons who might be physically defective, born with no feet, one arm or as Siamese twins, have perfectly intact souls. Their physical condition speaks nothing about their spiritual condition. They are still able to make right choices in their lives. But gay people are not. Our desires are so skewed, disordered and intrinsically evil that we must be told what to do and obey orders. That is not a tenable position. I don't even choose to argue with it particularly. These distant pronouncements have very little authority or reality to me—compared to the authority and reality of my life as I've lived it. I am not sick. I am not evil. The way I love is love. It took me twenty-five years to reach those conclusions, and the next twenty-five confirmed them.

"When gay people come out, they come out alone. So all the messages swirling around the atmosphere can be quite damaging at that point but I think the damage can be undone. Feeling you stand apart from the church may be a good thing, if it makes you question or if it leads you back to the roots of your faith. I would resist the idea of feeling too victimized by it. The church does worse by divorced and remarried Catholics, and all women, than it does by gay Catholics."

Patrick, who is fifty, was born in Oswego, a small town in upstate New York beside Lake Ontario. The inner recognition that he was gay had something to do with his quitting the church at the age of nineteen, but he said he might well have left then anyway. He still believed in God and wanted lead a spiritual life. But what he heard from the pulpit Sunday by Sunday seemed so condemnatory. Sermons inspired him as a child, but as a teenager they seemed sterile and lackluster. His grandmother had gone to Mass every day and had had a moral sense of what was right and what was wrong. One of the things he learned from her was that she lived by very strict rules—until they were broken by somebody she loved. Then she made a bit of an exception for them. For example, she hated people having long hair when they were in their twenties but, when Patrick did, she said it suited him.

"Our teachings come from our scripture and our traditions, represented to me by my grandparents, for example," he explained. "They emanate from how other people love, like my grandmother. That is how we know how God loves. And when you have been raised Catholic, it's as much a part of you as your teeth, hair or your fingernails. When it has been handed down to you by your ancestors, other ritual and systems of belief don't seem to have it quite right. My Catholicism was so deeply embedded in me that it was not quite compatible with any other denomination. My spirituality remained important to me but I wanted to wash my hands of organized religion because of uninformed, unintelligent positions it took."

During university years at Yale Patrick won a prize for short fiction. He thought he might become a poet until, during his "misspent youth" in New Orleans in his twenties, he ran into a group of actors "too cheap to pay royalties for any play they were producing." Discovering his literary talents, they invited him to write for them. So Patrick penned fifteen plays for the small company and almost all were performed. It felt like "an illicit pleasure" to be writing down words, then hearing people speaking them dramatically, creating on stage the world of his imagination.

Then one day, like the stuff of dreams, an influential television figure happened to be sitting in the audience. He was so impressed by the play that he contacted Patrick to see if he were interested in writing for a soap opera called *Search for Tomorrow*. It was the dawn of a television writing career which shone for twenty years, mainly through soaps and a couple of TV movies, carving him a reputation in the world of daytime television. In his early years as a scriptwriter, he was politically minded and, whenever there was an opportunity, he would try to slip in a gay character or correct stereotypical impressions about homosexuality.

At his peak he was responsible for two episodes of *General Hospital* every week. "I don't think there are half a dozen people on the planet who write two hours of television a week and it was never my ambition to be one of them," he told me. "I found myself screaming every time I answered the phone. I thought to myself, 'I can't do this any more. I'm near the top of this ladder but I don't see the benefit of scaling any more of it. I hate my life. I don't like being this person.' So I quit."

Patrick had been earning "a disgraceful amount of money" which he hadn't the time to spend. So he decided to sit back for a while and initiate his own writing projects.

But after the frenetic years of working in television, he suddenly found himself facing a number of personal crises and, for a while, everything seemed to spiral out of control. He experienced difficulties in his relationship, his mother was dangerously ill and, despite the security of his savings, he had no idea what to do with the rest of his life. Some people in a similar situation might have sought counseling but Patrick never felt his problems were psychological. After an absence of more than twenty years, he found his way back to the Catholic Church and to a congregation consisting largely of gay people. "I think people imagine that gay people flock to San Francisco and places like it so they can be gay, have wild sex and go to big parties with other gay people, or even hold jobs as teachers which they wouldn't be able to do back in their home towns. The reality is that you come to a place like this so you don't have to think about being gay. It just is. No one questions it. No one asks you about it. No one offends you. Going back to church, I felt the way any Catholic would after twenty years. I didn't feel gay and Catholic. I just felt Catholic."

It was the preaching of Father Tom Hayes—"a wonderful, gifted, funny homilist"—at Most Holy Redeemer in the Castro one day in 1994 that sealed Patrick's new journey. Father Tom talked passionately about morality without alluding to the acceptance and non-acceptance of anyone's sexuality. He addressed the congregation as adults—and made a deep impression on the forty-year-old. A couple of years later, Patrick's partner, Ken, got up one Sunday morning and announced that he was coming too. As Ken was not a Catholic, he went through the initiation program and was received into the Church. "It was a wonderful development in our relationship," said Patrick. "Our relationship is also enriched the experience of going to church. I love our congregation at Most Holy Redeemer because everyone in it has a running argument in their heads about whether they should be there at all. No one comes by accident or just because it's Sunday. There is a palpable feeling of commitment and prayerfulness—enough to curl your toes the first time you go. "Sometimes I think of us as the anti-Church church. We have a mission. When we have a new pastor or are visited by other priests, or by the archbishop, you know they think of us as a misguided bunch of people who should be brought more in line with the rest of the church. But we want the church to live up to our standard. They don't debate that. And instead of changing us, they may end up changed themselves. As a congregation, we sometimes quarrel, don't get along and can't decide what to do, just like other parish[es], but there is a community conversation that never ends. It's always about who God is, what God wants of us and how best to serve that."

Patrick initiated a homeless outreach program in the parish that he still runs. He says that, among the values he has inherited from the church of his childhood and from his own ancestors, is the notion that all people are "royalty in disguise." Everyone is homeless. The spiritual gifts of the people he now works with are "luxuriant and phenomenal in their variety and number." They need food, medicine, and shelter, but "we who are more privileged need what they have too." Patrick admitted that he had started out with the feeling that he was secure in his niche in the world, his church, his home and his relationship, so he could give something of that confidence back to the homeless. But he soon found out that God used vanity for God's own purposes. He learned more from the homeless than he could teach them. They were the church too. But he stressed that his work flowered from his humanity and not from any gay sensibility to journey with the marginalized. Indeed, he would be wary of claiming special insights, privileges, or spiritual development for gay and lesbian people. That seemed suspect to him. Being alongside the homeless had also spawned another genre of writing prose non-fiction through a fascination with the stories he heard and the people he met. He said such creativity emerged from a more genuine part of himself than the invention of scenarios for the heroes and heroines of *General Hospital*.

"I don't know what I would be like if I were not gay," Patrick added. "It's not something that has happened to me. It's been in me all my life, like Catholicism. I have no way to judge what I would be without it. But I don't consciously think about it. Twenty years ago Gore Vidal was telling us not to sign up for the word *gay*. He said there was no such thing as a gay person. At the time we thought he was being closeted and chicken. Now I know exactly what he meant.

A few months after this interview, the Mayor of San Francisco, Gavin Newsom, started dispensing marriage licenses for 4,000 same-sex couples. The action drew thousands from across the state and nation, and prompted similar action in other cities outside of California. I spoke to Patrick again and was surprised to discover that, despite his comments at the time of our original conversation, he and Ken had decided to get married at City Hall on February 26, 2004. "Of course it will all be declared null and void legally," he told me, "but we wanted to squeeze in before the courts call a halt. I remember telling you I didn't think Ken and I would race right down and sign up in the event 'gay marriage' became available. I guess I didn't know how I'd feel about it.

"A half-dozen young Japanese travelers were absolutely beside themselves about our wedding. They jumped up and down, took pictures of us, pumped our hands as excitedly as if we'd been the Mayor and First Spouse. Our friend Sheila, a Sister of Mercy, was one of our witnesses, and our atheist-Jewish friend Cynthia was the other. I had asked a priest friend if he would read the ceremony for us, since all that's required is that it be done by someone licensed in California to marry people, but his superiors had ordered him not to take part in any such abomination. (They were mostly worried about him being photographed, he said.) But he surprised us by showing up anyway, just to be there and watch. Everything about this has been surprising. Ken's eighty-six-year-old mother in Michigan can't stop calling to ask for details. She thinks our getting married is the best thing to happen since indoor heating.

"I will tell you the biggest surprise of all. I wasn't prepared for what it would feel like to stand there all by ourselves in City Hall's grand rotunda and say those same words people have used to pledge their love and faithfulness from time immemorial. Ken and I have been through other ceremonies, domestic-partner registration and so forth, as I told you. There was always something a little tinny and artificial about them, but we didn't mind. We just accepted those time-honored vows could never be spoken by couples like us. As I predicted to you, we held aloof from the first rush to City Hall. First we told ourselves the courts would stop it, then that the lines were too long and the weather too rotten to stand outside and wait. But I think the real reason was something else. People who keep canaries or cockatiels at home will tell you they can let the cage stand open and the dumb birds still won't fly away. God gave them wings but they've stopped thinking of using them. I didn't know how it would feel to be not 'married' but married, without the quotation marks. I've lived my whole life inside those quotation marks. I never knew how much they limited me until they were gone. To walk in the world without them is the most extraordinary feeling. The legal significance, whatever it turns out to be, is trivial compared to the human significance of what is happening here. I found my wings."

Then, in August 2004, the California Supreme Court did indeed rule that the mayor had usurped his authority by issuing the licenses. As part of its 5–2 decision, the court also nullified the licenses. These had been granted before the issuing of a court injunction to block the practice, pending a court review. The ruling stated: "We hold only that in the absence of a judicial determination that such statutory provisions are unconstitutional, local executive officials lacked authority to issue marriage licenses to solemnize marriages of, or register certificates of marriage for same-sex couples, and marriages conducted between same-sex couples in violation of the applicable statutes are void and of no legal effect."

The court did not, however, tackle the larger issue of whether the state's law prohibiting gay marriages, enacted by California voters through Proposition 22, was legal under the California constitution. The proposition states that marriage in California is defined as only between one man and one woman. I was curious to hear from Patrick more about the human impact of the court's action. "It was, of course, what I expected," he told me. "It would have been a miracle if it had gone the other way. Still, I'd be lying if I said I wasn't hoping for the miracle. There was an impromptu street rally in the neighborhood that night, which happens pretty reliably whenever something big comes down that affects us all, but I didn't feel up to going.

"That afternoon I ran into a friend on the street. I could see by his face he'd heard the news too. This is a wonderful guy, nice-looking man about my age, and it's been our way, in a certain humor, to be a little flirty—the sort of flirting you both know is not going anywhere, and you don't want it to. Everybody has at least one friendship like that. Anyway, I wanted to cheer him up, so I said, 'Good news—my marriage has just been annulled. I can fool around again!'

"That depressing little joke should be looked at carefully. People are always condemning or defending gay (male) promiscuity as though it were an eternal fact of our condition, but the alternate hypothesis has never been tested. The point sometimes makes its way into the same-sex marriage debate, in the rhetorical catch-22 form: 'You say our relationships aren't legitimate and then accuse us of being promiscuous. What's a homo to do?' I'm not sure anyone really gets the connection the way the old missionaries did. 'We were horrified by the savages' indiscriminate acts of lewdness. But now, having taught them the sacredness of the nuptial bond, and having performed marriages among the converts, it is touching to witness the mutual devotion of the new spouses.'

"No doubt people will try to console us by saying the distinction's just imaginary. What does it matter what the law says? You can be as married as you want to be, in your own minds! No. No, we can't. I understand that now in a way I never did before; I suppose all eight thousand of us who were married here do. Telling two people that God and the state affirm an interest in their love and faithfulness is not a psychological trick you can perform on yourself at home. There is no such thing as 'just as good as married.'

"Ken and I have never felt more like a family than in the last month. An actual wedding present arrived. It's the only one we got, except for the roses Ken's mom sent, and it's from people I hardly know, but it's sitting in the middle of the dining room like a trophy. A young couple in the homeless program I run had a baby on the fourth of July, Independence Day. He was baptized in our church a couple of Sundays ago. I'm his godfather. He's cranky and messy, all appetite and poop, so I've been taking him now and then to give the new parents a break. He fell asleep on my chest one night, listening to my heartbeat. I could smell his milky breath and milk-made skin. I could hear Ken snoring. It was dark and the house felt full of safety and sweetness. A middle-aged married guy babysitting his godson, lying awake and thinking how good life is.

"Some of that's already starting to slip away. I'm fighting like hell to hold onto it, but that old feeling is seeping back in, like gas. Those quotation marks I told you about—I can feel them descending again. Do we have to go back to the status of kids in the yard playing house? 'Isn't that cute, you children go right on playing.' They can believe in their tables and teacups all they want, but their house has no roof and no doors.

"That's not even the right analogy for us now. Unless you suppose the kids in the yard really had a house once—the doors, the roof, the shelves, the creaky step. They remember every inch of the way it was before the fire, the eviction, the flood. Their make-believe isn't fantasy. They're trying to conjure it back.

"It's odd to be declared invalid. At the same time, there's a—I wouldn't call it relief; a relaxation, maybe. It's familiar. The suspense is over. The great thing did not last, and after all these years, being invalid is our special expertise. We know well enough how to go back to it. The difference is, this time we won't go willingly. City Hall is offering to give us our money back—it cost us, what, a hundred bucks to get married, in fees and what not. It's like a consumer recall. 'Dear Customer: Due to circumstances beyond our control, your radial tires have been found defective, please return to your authorized dealer for a full refund.' We don't want a refund, and we don't want the old treadless tires back. We just got the new ones on and they were taking us where we wanted to go.

"Here is something I'm not proud of. A straight friend of mine just got married. I love him dearly, but I ignored his wedding, just as he ignored mine, and since the ruling I've ticked off at him, completely unreasonably. He didn't make the rules. He would probably change them if he could. But he's not about to give up his own seat in the front of the bus. And why should he? Six months ago that kind of thinking would never have occurred to me. I don't like resentment, it's ugly, and I will rid myself of it before I see him again. It's not his happiness I resent, of course. I just don't understand why he can't see me over here in the corner, a guy he's known and cared about for over twenty years, why it doesn't matter to him that the bouncers won't let me in. The promises Meg is making to him no one's allowed to make to me. Somebody tried to, and the President, the Governor, the highest court in California all stepped in with loudspeakers to assure everybody they didn't count.

"Never mind the tax and insurance and legal advantages gay people are denied because we can't marry. They may have made for a winning argument in Massachusetts, but I don't give a hoot about those things. What I want is the authenticity that being married confers. Or to say the same thing another way, the ordinariness.

"I was never a same-sex-marriage activist until now. Being married without quotation marks made me one. You can't show me what I've been living without, then take it away and tell me to go play house. They can keep our hundred bucks. We're keeping our marriage license. And I'm not sending that wedding present back."

three

Saints and Shepherds

When Canon Gene Robinson became the first openly gay priest in the Anglican Communion to be consecrated a bishop, he told the congregation that the ceremony was not about him. "It's about so many other people who find themselves at the margins and for whatever reason have not known the ear of the Lord's favor," he said. "Our presence here is a welcome sign for those people to be brought into the center."

More than four thousand people gathered in the late afternoon of Sunday, November 2, 2003, to witness the consecration of the 993rd bishop of the Episcopal Church of the United States of America. It was also the festival of All Saints. Hundreds of priests, altar boys and girls, and lay people with banners walked in procession through the Whittemore Center at the University of New Hampshire as an organist and silver band played with rousing enthusiasm and the voices of a massed choir reached to the heavens. Above the ceremony, a darting paper dove, symbolizing the movement of the Holy Spirit, pierced the fragrant air. Gene Robinson was consecrated by fifty-six bishops to the aroma of freshly burning incense and to the acoustic of traditional hymnody including "For all the Saints," "Amazing Grace," "All People That on Earth Do Dwell," and "The Church's One Foundation" with its verse about the church being "by schism rent asunder, by heresies distressed."

The election had already been affirmed by the Episcopal Church's General Convention and nearly two hundred church leaders of all Christian denominations from across the state of New Hampshire had expressed their support. But some Episcopal parishes swiftly formed alternative allegiances, while others agreed to withhold contributions to diocesan funds in protest at the consecration of the fifty-six-year-old priest who has a long-term male partner.

"As hands were laid on him that day, there was total, prayerful exuberance on my part," said the Reverend Joseph Lane, who was among the clergy who donned vestments and wore labels declaring "I'm proud to be an Episcopalian." In the congregation sat Joseph's partner, Jay Framson. He was sporting a badge proclaiming, "Jews for Gene." Jay grew up in an Orthodox Jewish household. Even though he no longer practices his faith, this was not a time to disown his religious credentials.

"The consecration felt like coming home," Joseph reflected. "It carried for so many of us the sense that we really are welcome in this church and we are who we really are." It had been a drizzly afternoon in New Hampshire and people had been forced to undergo airport-like security searches because of the death threats Gene Robinson had received. But Joseph said he had been "as proud as punch" for the entire day and could not be bothered with the placard-waving "God Hates Fags" contingent. In any event, there had been specific support by students who were proclaiming an alternative message, "Gay? Fine By Us." Joseph had seen people shouting at each other but he hadn't felt like joining in. He was too busy "being thrilled with the event of the day."

Back at the Good Shepherd Episcopal Church in Belmont, California, Joseph told me that he believed Gene Robinson would prove to be "an extraordinary bishop" because of his many pastoral and spiritual gifts. They flowered irrespective of his sexual orientation. He did not, however, dispute the suggestion that Bishop Robinson brought specific insights to the episcopal ministry by virtue of his being gay. The consecration symbolized the fact that all people, including homosexuals, were called to be saints of God. The same sentiment was reflected on a banner hanging outside Joseph's church. Its white lettering against a blue background read, "Join us around a table where we are all welcome for ever!"

Joseph and Jay, an attorney, are completely open about their relationship. They share their home with Ellie, a German shepherd, and Oliver the cat. Jay turns up at parish events as the rector's partner and displays affection as appropriate. "Some people think I wear my sexuality on my sleeve," Joseph confessed. "Why is it fine for a heterosexual clergy couple to hold hands but, when Jay and I do it, we're flaunting our relationship?"

The couple met at a gay bar in San Francisco. "He didn't say he was a priest the first time we met," Jay disclosed. "But when we were planning our first date, then he told me. I wasn't shocked but I was surprised because I had no idea. If you're in a relationship with a priest, you have to be prepared to deal with certain issues, such as having all the parishioners in your life and having to meet and greet people a lot. I accepted that as I went along with the relationship. It doesn't present problems but it's different from other relationships I have been in. If I hadn't wanted to assume the role I now have, I wouldn't have gone deeper into the relationship. I'm a former English and journalism student. I worked on newspapers for several years before going to law school. So being the partner of a priest offers me an interesting vantage point from which to observe people. And they're always fascinating."

Taking me on a tour of the wood-built church, with its stations of the cross nailed outside on a veranda, Joseph said he could not envisage himself in a situation where he had to hide his partnership. Nearing his fiftieth birthday, he was too old for that. If Jay had not shown any interest in being part of parish life, he would have honored that decision. But if members of the congregation had ever indicated that Jay was not welcome at parish functions or was not included in the dinner invitations, Joseph would have had a harder time dealing with it. For him, it was a simple matter of integrity, although he did not judge as less virtuous those gay priests who lived more secretly than he did. He said he grieved for homosexuals who had to hide who they were. He could not be a priest if he had to disguise his sexual identity.

"I do my best to be as sensitive as I can to people who feel uncomfortable with my being gay," he said. "I have my own feelings of anger about having to justify my existence but I am prepared to have conversations—often very naked conversations—in order to help people along. It's really hard, however, to have that conversation with someone who does not think I should be at the Lord's Table or with somebody who thinks I ought to be dead. A reasonable extension of comments like 'You're going to go to hell' is that you are already dead."

From childhood, Joseph sensed he had a vocation to lead a congregation. He was raised in a Southern Baptist family in Pine Bluff, Arkansas. The one-time trombonist had "a slow-paced southern upbringing" during the civil rights era when his family was known for being more liberal and progressive on racial issues than many of their contemporaries. Joseph's parents divorced when he was six but he "continued to be the church mouse."

As a college student, he dated a girl for three years and got involved in a "romp 'em, stomp 'em" Southern Baptist campus church. He was no stranger to fundamentalist groups like The Navigators or Campus Crusade for Christ. He remembered how they always condemned sex outside of marriage and how some of his male friends felt obliged to stand up at church gatherings and "testify to their wicked ways." In those days, Joseph found it easy to buy into the ethic of a platonic relationship. It was only after he had left college that he came into contact with the local gay community and began to accept his sexual identity, of which he had been only dimly aware. "Some definition to those underlying emotions and feelings were given form then," he told me.

Joseph had planned to go to Dallas Theological Seminary (one of the most conservative fundamentalist schools in the United States) with a view to becoming the minister of a Baptist church or an independent congregation. Aware of his obesity, he decided to lose weight and transform his appearance. He started jogging in a neighborhood. His daily circuit happened to take him through a park that, unbeknown to him, was a meeting place for gay men. He felt a curious attraction to this covert world. But there was an immediate conflict between this apparent confirmation of his sexual identity and the anti-homosexual teachings of his fundamentalist church. Initially he decided to turn his back on his sexuality, telling his new gay pals that he wouldn't be seeing them any more. One of them laughed in his face and said Joseph would be back in about two weeks. He was.

Paradoxically, however, it was his Baptist upbringing that eventually gave him the spiritual courage to own who he was. His pastors had instilled in him the belief that "once saved, always saved." He already felt confident as a child of God and believed he was accepted by God, even though his being gay remained entirely at odds with the conservative religious environment of his youth. "I held those two aspects of myself together and believed they would balance out," he said. "I knew who I was as a human being created in God's image. Like Mary, I held these things in my heart. I still use a lot of blue in my vestments to remind me of Mary."

But the road to ordination was long indeed. Joseph put his vocation on hold for fifteen years, becoming a sales representative for the design and gift industries. He also helped as a volunteer with the AIDS Foundation in Houston before moving to San Francisco to work full time for a major AIDS organization. It was the time when those with AIDS-related illnesses did not want to be classed as victims but as people living with HIV/AIDS. "I, too, have chosen not to be a victim but that's not to say I have never been victimized," he pointed out. "There is now a sense of self-empowerment about my life, although not in the form of triumphalism."

When Joseph decided to join the Episcopal Church, thoughts of ordination recurred. But he was adamant that he could only ever work in a diocese where he could bring the whole of who he was to the ministry. By then the major psychological conflict within him had subsided. He decided to be open about his homosexuality at every stage of the selection procedure. "In my initial interview with the bishop, I was asked if I were promiscuous," he explained. "I told the bishop that I enjoyed dating, valued good ethical relationships and did not feel I was called to be celibate. I was ordained on that basis. My bishop made it clear that he looked for people who were honest and healthy. Hopefully he sensed that in me."

Always nursing a desire to be a rector, Joseph eventually applied for a vacancy at the Church of the Good Shepherd. It was a small congregation and had not participated in the human sexuality debates. Yet when he arrived for the interview, the parishioners seemed to know he was gay. Word had already spread that the shortlist was composed of two women and one gay man. Joseph was offered the job. The issue of his being gay had, in fact, been discussed with the parish before he arrived, so he was spared the ordeal of coming out to the congregation. But not all its members have been at ease with his openness. Jay told me that, even though most worshipers there were straight, Joseph's honesty had particularly assisted him in his relationships with gay parishioners. "I can't really say how I think his being gay helps him, or even affects, his ministry," he remarked. "It's just one more piece of the tapestry that makes up who he is. I guess the question of how his being gay affects his ministry makes as little sense to me as asking how another priest's being straight might affect his ministry."

Joseph is president of the diocesan gay, lesbian, transgender and bisexual organization, Oasis/California and is involved in the leadership of Claiming the Blessing, a national movement working toward the passage of a resolution authorizing the development of liturgies for same-sex unions in the Episcopal Church. Joseph has bestowed blessings on two couples living outside the parish. He said he had prepared them as he would a heterosexual couple planning a marriage.

"For me the act of blessing affirms something that is already true and that somehow makes it more real experientially, although it does not make it more true," he observed. "I think a comparison could be made with the act of baptism. When you baptize someone, they nominally become a Christian but I believe that person was already beloved and accepted by God. In the same way, although we have not had our own relationship blessed, I think God has already blessed the life we share each day."

four

Guarded Secrets

"I feel terrified—more frightened than ever before," said Kay, looking up from the cluster of newspaper articles, magazines and Sunday supplements which had accumulated in the kitchen since the Jeffrey John case hit the headlines. "A great evil has been unleashed and is abroad."

Kay admitted that she now felt unsafe. It was a few weeks after Southwark Cathedral's canon theologian had been forced to withdraw from his appointment as the next Bishop of Reading following pressure from evangelicals objecting to his stance on homosexuality. "I always thought such a force was out there," said Kay. "Now I know that the force also has a face and a voice, an enemy that has gained power and control. I know, at a very profound level, that I am definitely not safe. I am no longer secure—even if I ever were."

Kay is an Anglican priest who secretly shares her parish home with her lesbian partner, Louise, who is also a priest, a situation officially forbidden by the Church of England. If priests who were celibate and gay (such as Jeffrey John) could not be protected, there could be no safe havens for clergy like them, they explained. Kay said she lived in constant fear, a state of mind that absorbed time and energy in trying not to appear paranoid or too neurotic. She had to monitor her own behavior and other people's reactions so her cover would not be blown. She had to maintain "a politically astute eye" on every occasion, even having to assess her likely responses to straightforward questions before she dared answer.

"I have become a guarded person—and I don't think that is healthy or holy," Kay told me. "I feel I am two people—the public priest and the private individual. I martyr the truth of myself. I go to great lengths to leave people wondering, when it would be so much easier for me and for everybody else just to be straightforward, honest and truthful. The truth and the dishonesty of living a life, and not appearing to live out of the lie of it, but out of the truth of it, is very difficult to sustain."

The couple said they had felt badly let down by the events of 2003 and their relationship has since been under great strain. While Kay did not think she could ever abandon her vocation as a priest, Louise felt like resigning her orders. She said she had been devastated by Jeffrey John's forced withdrawal. She knew him by reputation. He was exactly the sort of person who should be a bishop. She had not the slightest interest in whether or not he had ever had a partner and was "outraged" that he had had to make assurances about his private life.

"I was hopeful that Archbishop Rowan Williams and the rest would have brazened this out," she sighed. "Who knows what a price Jeffrey John has paid himself for all this? It is shocking that a minority section of the church can hold the rest to ransom in this way. Since the announcement that Jeffrey John was standing down, I have had a real struggle as to whether I can actually remain in the church as a priest."

Louise felt the church had betrayed a complete lack of understanding, resulting in "an objectification almost of gay people." It had pushed out homosexuals to the margins so they could be observed dispassionately, "almost as a different form of human being." There was "a real neuroticism" about how people related to each other physically. The undercurrent to the present debate revealed a deep anxiety about something which had very little to do with the lives of gay people and their relationships. When the churches talked about the needs of gay people, they always started from a position that implied gay people had completely different requirements from everybody else, such as special support for their relationships. Louise said she had always wanted to respond by explaining that gay people were simply human beings who loved others like everybody else. They formed life-long bonds and often led ordinary lives. As Christians, they did not need new strategies or approaches.

Both regarded their sexuality and their priesthood as inseparable. "I actually think my sexuality has only become a wound because of my vocation as a priest," Louise said. "I don't think that, in itself, my sexuality is a wound. But in the context of the church it is." There was the lack of an environment in which to explore sexual identity openly. There were few safe havens where they could talk without inhibition about the nature of relationships, how they were formed and how they were broken. Many lesbians had become strong women because such fortitude had emerged passionately from their conviction, experience, and sense of persecution. "This particular lesbian is a strong woman and nobody's fool," Kay insisted. "She will stand up to whomever she comes up against, look them in the eye and dare them to go further." Kay said she shared a lot of similarities with her mother, who was a strong woman, "but not in quite the same way as I am now." She thought something of her experience as a gay woman had forged that steeliness. For Louise, sharing a home and a life with Kay had brought into focus a determination and confidence about handling herself in situations where she might feel under threat of attack.

The wound of homosexuality was not "nurse-able" as such, said Louise, preferring to talk about its transformation which she thought would eventually occur because "the basic right is on our side." Societies were moving toward greater inclusiveness. There had been increasing acceptance of minorities and of difference, although it had been "a very painful journey." The open ministry of gay people would emerge in time because so many were fighting for it. But it was still a long way off.

Gay people brought to the priesthood "the same sorts of gifts" as other individuals called to ministry. But for Louise, the particular experience of being gay in the church at this time gave "a certain grit," creating something that could be offered back. Too often the church expressed itself through an institution or hierarchy. This had obscured its more prophetic role on the edge. A firm grounding on the margins, which gay priests had experienced historically, was crucial for any deep understanding of ministry. Over the past 150 years, many gay priests in Anglo-Catholic parishes had often worked in the toughest areas. It was a Christ-like vocation to feed this experience of marginality back to those at the heart of the institution, such as those clerics accustomed to ministering in more comfortable parishes. They had a tendency to make false assumptions about the integrity of gay priests working in inner-city areas.

When Louise originally told her former parish priest (a woman) that she was in a relationship with Kay, the priest remarked, "Isn't it extraordinary how, despite the church, God keeps on calling gay people to be priests? I never fail to marvel at it." But it was often a struggle, maintained Louise, to come to an acceptance of a sexual identity that was not the norm, one that did not easily have many ready-made role models. If a woman could reach a position where she could accept herself as a lesbian or had entered a same-sex relationship, she had probably done a greater amount of work on herself and a greater degree of "thinking through" than a straight person. Heterosexuals might never make that critical journey toward self-knowledge.

As a naturally open and gregarious individual, Louise said she struggled with the lack of honesty that inevitably clouded her pastoral relationships. She was someone who could talk naturally about her life and what was important to her, so she had had to learn to be circumspect. This had been "incredibly damaging" in the context of her priesthood, hampering her relationships with people, especially in the parish where she was unable to share the whole of who she was. She imagined the congregation thinking, "There's something about this woman that we don't know—she's a little cagey about what she does with her time off."

From the moment Kay began to form her own identity as an adult, it was in the context of knowing that she was lesbian. When, at the age of seventeen, she realized she had fallen in love for the first time and it happened to be with a woman, she sensed that, no matter the pattern of the rest of her life, that one experience had placed her on the edge, where nothing could ever be secure or predictable again. Being in that exposed, yet hidden, place necessitated a watchfulness that could sometimes produce feelings of paranoia. Words from the Anglican service of Compline were often in her thoughts: "Be sober, be vigilant; because your adversary the devil, as a roaring lion, walketh about, seeking whom he may devour: whom resist, steadfast in the faith" (1 Peter 5:8, 9).

Kay confessed, "I am constantly looking at where I am and asking, 'Who am I?' and 'Where is God in this?' It is a vocation that always costs all. You recognize the vulnerability of the place where, by chance, you have found yourself in the world. But that is also a potential strength; it makes me take the whole understanding of vocation with a huge seriousness. It's desperately important to me. I think the calling forth of an individual, a human being, has to be constant and there are those who misunderstand the idea of vocation as being a one-off concept. They think, 'I *have been* called and I am *now* called. Everything is all right.' That sort of model of priestly vocation is characteristic of ministry within the institution but less so in a community of people who know themselves to be vulnerable." Although Kay had never gone through a period of self-hatred, she said it took courage every day "to remain true and honest." But within that risk-taking, she saw God calling her forth and drawing her onward.

The disguises, however, had to stay on. Kay's mask was her dog collar, she told me, worn always as a guard. She wished she were the sort of priest who could take off the collar regularly but she knew that "in the very doing up of that tight collar," she was keeping herself in check. But when she felt free to take off the collar, she could relax—and that was usually not until she was safely indoors. It was "a deeply unhealthy way" of being a priest or a human being. "I am this particular sort of priest because I am a lesbian," she continued. "It has something to do with having an affinity with the wounded and the marginalized. It is also about enabling others to make sense of their journey. I want to be standing at the door of the church, holding it open and saying, 'You might have thought you wouldn't be welcome here but actually you are.' That is not just an expression of my theology of priesthood. People walk into the church and stay because of that attitude."

This representational model of priesthood, where visitors *presumed* the woman at the altar was a lesbian (without having evidence), encouraged like-minded Christians to celebrate who *they* were without having to make a point about it. People neither desired nor needed to make such bold statements but there might be an awareness that, even if they were not absolutely convinced that the priest before them was a lesbian, at the deepest level of connection, they were sufficiently confident of the fact to feel comfortable. Kay said her rule of thumb was not to mention her sexual orientation unless a specific pastoral need necessitated it.

"But it is a huge risk all the same," she pointed out. "It would be no different from revealing to them that I had been sexually abused. The sexually abused come to me because they know that, at some level, I will be a safe person for them to be with. In the course of these pastoral encounters, I often wonder if they need to know that I understand them from specific personal experience. And, if so, should I say, 'Yes I do?' In the main I don't because it isn't necessary. I think a connection takes place without the naming."

Being lesbian was "utterly good and wonderful, a blessing in my life," Kay confirmed. And her relationship with Louise was *the* blessing of her life, "the most life-giving, wonderful and lovely thing." But the friendship had originally come as a complete surprise. Having just ended a long-term relationship, Kay had been neither looking for nor expecting another, especially as she was in training for priesthood. "I was pretty convinced I would have to remain a single person if I wanted to continue in the church as a priest," she said. "Not only was I not looking for a relationship but I missed the obvious because of that. When I finally realized what was happening at theological college, that I was falling in love with somebody who was also falling in love with me, I was completely overwhelmed by that extraordinary, unexpected, unasked for, undeserved gift. That, I think, is the nature of blessing. One can never earn blessing or work toward it. By its very nature it is free, unasked for and overly generous and extraordinary—pressed down and running over."

Louise agreed that, fundamentally, homosexuality was a blessing, even if, at this time in the history of the Anglican Communion, it was difficult to feel quite so positive. The relationship helped her minister more effectively because being with Kay had enabled her to become the person she was meant and called to be. This sense of completion and fulfillment overflowed into everything she did. The paradox lay in the fact that the blessing, which bestowed on her the depth to be the priest she was, was also a wound containing within it the very impediments to an open and honest ministry.

Because they had met at theological college, their whole formation as priests had taken place within their own relationship. The two worlds were entwined and enriching of one another. "We don't really know how to be priests outside this relationship," said Louise. "And we don't know how to be in this relationship without being priests," Kay added. "But, at the moment, the church is a very unsafe place for us to be and is giving our relationship its severest test."

five

Through the Whispering Darkness

"It's better to love and be attracted, than to hate and kill," proclaimed award-winning Christian poet Rowland Macaulay. "I'm a very sensual person and I'm thankful to God for creating me homosexual."

Rowland is a people-loving performer whose blend of music, dance and drama has enlivened theatres around the world. His unique African style of poetic ministry has won him popular acclaim as he seeks to "spread the good news of the Lord Jesus Christ" through his work. He has published widely too. But few readers of his poems would realize that his stanzas have been inspired by his gay identity as well as his religious convictions. Here is an example of his sexuality and his spirituality interconnecting in verse:

> *When my mind no longer touches my soul*
> *My soul cried at night*
> *Begging the whispering darkness*
> *To identify my personality*
> *Snoring like a hibernating bear*
> *Unaware of my winter*[1]

"A lot of what I have written in my poems is very well hidden within my pain and, when I revisit them, they relieve some of the anguish I have gone through," he told me in a bar in South East London, close to where he is a self-employed business consultant.

"My writings and daily experiences are sermons in development. I would like to become the author of books that will change people for life. I want to reach them with all my inner thoughts. God knows I have so much love to give."

Admitting his homosexuality to himself was difficult enough. But the self-disclosure led to the ending of his marriage, death threats and anxiety over the care of his son. In the end Rowland suffered a breakdown. "It took the grace of God for me to go through it and come out of it alone," he explained. "The Bible says God will not give us a burden we cannot get out of. I just believe that some of my pain has been for a reason. I trust God. I thank him for those pains because, when I am going through them, I have no control. But thankfully I am still here and able to talk about it."

Born in Islington, North London, in 1965, Rowland was brought up in Nigeria, where he moved with his parents when he was three. They introduced him to Jesus. From an early age, he loved the church and the Bible. He later became a Pentecostal Christian but, in 1998, was ordained a minister in Christian Soul Winners, founded by his father, a leading Nigerian theologian. A non-denominational organization, it trains ministers, teachers, church managers and pastoral-care workers. One of its wings is the United Bible University in Lagos, of which his father is president.

"I have been gay since the day I was born," he continued. "The awareness came when I was about eleven but there was very little I could do about it. I was quite effeminate. I remember my grandmother telling me to stand properly and not like a girl. I was quite confused because I didn't know how girls stood. I only knew how *I* stood. But I tried to stand properly after that.

"I suppressed my sexuality which is not to say I did not experience it. I did—with other teenage boys my age. But because of my faith as a Christian, I wasn't very confident about my sexuality. I didn't understand it. I was so confused about it. I think the homosexual person really needs to have some counseling. It is important that people come to understand their sexuality when they are young. I suffered a lot from a very tender age because I thought there was something wrong with me—that I was sick, an abomination and that God hated me. Every time I responded to my sexual feelings, I ended up having to ask God for forgiveness. I prayed for sanctification. I wanted to purify myself. I never celebrated my sexuality. My sexuality was a big part of me but I was not a big part of my sexuality."

As reactions in Nigeria to the consecration of Gene Robinson have shown, the country remains fiercely opposed to homosexuality. There is no form of pastoral care for gay men and women, who are often left wondering if the acute isolation they experience is felt only by them. Homosexual friendships of any kind are strictly forbidden. Anyone found guilty could be imprisoned for fourteen years. Subsidiary regulations infringe on gay rights and other liberties.

Nigeria is "backwards" in its acceptance of sexual difference because of its cultural values and tradition, says Rowland. Families are always worried about their reputations if it becomes known a child of theirs is gay. There is also a complete lack of understanding about human rights. Gay and lesbian Christian movements are forced to operate under total secrecy. "You go to a meeting without telling anyone else where you're going," he explained. "The majority of my friends and contacts in Nigeria are actually married men who still practice homosexuality. If you are a male child in your family, you are expected to get married."

Like many young Africans, Rowland received his education and training from his parents. Returning to the United Kingdom, he decided to go to university and immersed himself in the life of a Nigerian community in London. Rowland met the woman who would become his wife at a Pentecostal church. "This was with some knowledge of my sexuality, even though I had spent my entire life trying to suppress it," he acknowledged. "I had never thought that, if I got married, my sexuality would go away. I had always thought my sexual practice in the past with another man had been a sin. I have been at prayer meetings where they have asked people to pray especially against the spirit of homosexuality. I would sit there, but God knew I was not taking part in those prayers. I was sometimes challenged about why I was not praying. I simply told them that I did not have a burden to pray against the spirit of homosexuality. That would have taken away the principle of the love Christ has asked us to practice."

Rowland and his girlfriend married in 1991 and had one son, but they were divorced in 1994. "I said to my wife one day that I had something to tell her—that I was gay," he recalled. "She was very, very surprised. She said she couldn't compete with that side of me. I didn't regret the marriage because I had entered into it with very little understanding of my true sexuality and I did enjoy the relationship. We had a fantastic time. When I came to tell her I was gay, I was going through a psychological breakdown. I was depressed. A lot was happening to me that I could not explain. Telling her was a confession of truth. If I had not said I was gay at the time, I would have been living a double life or lying to her.

"After that, we had a good relationship for about three months until she eventually told her family. Then all hell broke loose and the repercussions were very difficult. Her brothers threatened me. They were going to kill me. They were going to batter my face if anything happened to their sister. I think they acted out of absolute ignorance and lack of understanding. Then they tried to take my son away from me. I was quite worried so I took out a court order to ensure he wouldn't be taken out of the country. If that had happened, I wouldn't have seen him again. I did love my ex-wife and I think she is a wonderful person. But the breakdown became acrimonious because of how it was handled. It was a high climax of unhappiness. What any of them might have done was unimaginable. I did a number of things I wasn't proud of as well. Everybody was fighting for what they felt they should fight for and I was fighting to make sure my son remained in the United Kingdom. The stakes were high."

Rowland said he had failed to receive any support whatsoever from the church he was attending at the time, even though he was in need of immense pastoral and spiritual care. He was a member of the leadership team but was abruptly cold-shouldered. "I was really surprised by that," he said. "There was a friend in the church who knew I was gay. When I told him I was going to have to get a divorce, he told me that, if I did, I should not talk to him again. Ten years on, he still hasn't spoken to me. Nobody wanted to talk to me any longer. I was more or less an outcast as far as the church was concerned. It had a serious impact on me. I stopped going to church for a number of years. But, because of my love for Jesus and my Christian faith, I was able to focus on my relationship to God in a one-to-one way until I found another church. But by then I didn't want to start having to explain my sexuality, so I began to lead a double life. I lied. I was one person in the church and another person outside. Although I didn't admit I was gay, it was only a matter of time before I was found out."

A few years ago, Rowland agreed to take part in a British television documentary which examined the lives of homosexuals from African-Caribbean backgrounds who had put down roots in the United Kingdom. As he was still an active member of a Pentecostal church, he indicated to the producers that he was concerned about his identity being revealed. Even though he felt it important to be truthful, he did not want to embarrass his son. Furthermore, he was concerned how his church community might react if it realized one of its most prominent members was openly homosexual. So Rowland asked to be interviewed in silhouette but, when the program was broadcast early in 2000, he was horrified to discover that his features hadn't been adequately disguised. The church members were sure to recognize him. They did.

"I received a phone call from the pastor, who told me that what I was doing was evil," Rowland told me. "Everything I was afraid of came to be. I was given books to read which told me my homosexuality was wrong. I was invited to three meetings where there was an attempt to exorcise me and change my sexuality. You can't be healed from homosexuality, despite the propaganda perpetrated by certain churches. When people used to pray against the spirit of homosexuality, I always wondered why it had no effect on me!

"I even went through a period when I had to give an account of my sexual relationships, mentioning the people with whom I'd had sex and where it had happened. I was made to confess every single sexual experience I had taken part in. It was terrible. Horrific. After the third meeting, I didn't tell the pastor I wouldn't be attending those sessions any more. I still kept going to the church but I met so many barriers. I had been an active member of the art and media group but I was no longer welcomed in the team. I also wanted to become one of the youth leaders but my services were not welcomed. It was all an indirect way of forcing me out so in the end I decided not to go to the church any more."

In December 2002 Rowland ended his association with the Pentecostal movement and began to make enquiries on the Internet about gay Christian churches and discovered the Metropolitan Community Church. "As I am not in a relationship as such, I think I can focus more on my responsibilities as a gay Christian leader," he enthused. "For me that is a source of encouragement and empowerment. I have gone through right of membership of MCC and been confirmed as a member of the church. I started clergy training in 2004 and plan to have my clergy status transferred to the MCC at the end of my training. I believe there are more conferences to speak at, more platforms to climb and more people for me to unburden and release from their captivity. I know I can do this through the grace of God and the strength given to me. My parents brought me up as a person to love Jesus and that love does not change. But I think I now feel more comfortable with my sexuality and more outspoken about it. I am a freer person because of it, but I think that is presenting a new problem for my family."

It is perhaps not surprising therefore that it was only in September 2003 that Rowland summoned the courage to talk about his sexuality with his father. During the conversation, his father expressed how much he loved Rowland but it was apparent he had no understanding of or support for his son's sexuality. "I think that is the only thing that hurts," said Rowland. "My father recently wrote me a letter in which he said I had joined a satanic group—the gay community—and that I should get out of it and come back to Jesus. But I still love my father and I have so much sympathy for him as well.

"My Christian faith has been unshaken through this. I have studied theology up to master's level and he trained me as well. It was really painful for him to realize that his lovely, reliable child was gay. What was painful for me was when he said in his letter that people were going to lose respect and integrity for me. If that were the case, they never had any respect for me in the first place.

"We are still on talking terms but I think my sexuality remains a very, very delicate area. My mum is very understanding but, because of the culture, I am sure she wishes she did not have a gay child. My relationship with her hasn't changed. It's very difficult to say whether or not my brothers and sisters know because they won't talk about it. I guess they will have found out somehow and I suspect they told my father."

Rowland still sees his son regularly but laments the fact that he has lost a good many friends in recent years. "I think they find me a dangerous person because they are still conforming to the African culture and the black people's culture. Some of them said they would support me but, when it came to it, they were nowhere to be found. I am not surprised. Jesus Christ had twelve disciples and how many were beside him as he went to be crucified? I identify with him. It is a very lonely world."

A long-standing love of Scripture has inspired Rowland to reread the Bible from cover to cover, concentrating on the passages in the Old and New Testaments that contain references to homosexuality. By studying the interpretations of scholars, he has been able to offer his own informed opinions. "As an individual I can tell the difference between wrong and right," he said. "I did not think my sexuality was something that was wrong, so I used to turn around and blame God. But God is omnipotent and omniscient, so how could I really blame him for it? Now I praise and thank him. If there had been more understanding and more knowledge about sexuality from a younger age, I believe I would have made a decision to be gay from the outset without thinking it was a sin. What I needed was an education on morals and how to get into good relationships from the beginning."

Rowland felt, however, that he could draw on the African experience in a positive way because of the years he had spent living in Nigeria. He knew the expectations of the African child—and the expectations of the culture too. Parents in Nigeria believed they could lean on their children's reputation as a form of empowerment for them. But that could be extremely psychologically damaging, especially for gay children whose fathers had reputations to protect. "In future I know that, if ever I meet an African child who is gay, I will be able to identify with their situation and what they have been through," he said. "I will be able to pass on the good news that Jesus loves them and tell them that it's okay to be gay—and it's okay to be Christian.

"I think my sexuality is undoubtedly a gift from God—and it has taken me too long to say that."

Love must start at home before going abroad
You must be able to look in the mirror
And say, you did a good job

I will not settle for anyone
That gives me what I am incapable of giving myself
I am not arrogant but I need to strike a healthy balance
Somewhere between martyrdom and narcissism

I noticed every other person's needs are more important than mine
Then I end up resentful, living without a thing
With no self respect, living to please another
Because I thought I was worth nothing

Usually I melt at the incapable looks
One critical look disengaged my strand
And narrows my dreams
Insecure and vulnerable

I see myself as settled and stabilized
I sing aloud my own songs
I will train you how to treat me
In friendship, harmony, opulence and tenderness

Now, I believe in myself
I respect my own opinions
Admiration for my feelings
I show consideration for my judgments[2]

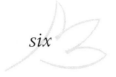

six

Madness and Passion

The psychoanalyst looked the priest straight in the face. "I want to be really clear with you," he said.

Sebastian held his breath. This was the moment of truth. He had been sent to the clinic by the head of his religious order whose harsh words were still ringing in his ears—"I think you are mad."

The superior's abrupt diagnosis had come as a shock, for Sebastian's parishioners considered him one of the sanest priests they had ever known. Eager to communicate the social dimension of the Gospel, Sebastian had seemed to unite Catholics of all ages. The elderly, especially, loved him. So did many others. Young people had started coming to church again because his radical style of preaching connected with their experience.

Now he found himself under scrutiny at a center noted for its work in counseling clergy who had abused children or drank too much—on trial for the "madness" of addressing the issues of sexual abuse and HIV/AIDS in his homilies. Following an intensive week of psychological tests and interviews, he felt both drained and humiliated. After all, only a few years before, the same provincial had singled out Sebastian as "the best hope for this religious congregation in years." Sebastian wondered if he was about to be designated "too insane for the pulpit."

Staring back at the analyst, the priest braced himself for the worst. Judgment came swiftly.

"There's absolutely nothing wrong with you, psychologically or emotionally," Sebastian was informed. "In fact, you are a fine, balanced young man. Your problem is this: your provincial thinks you are gay. If you are, he has a problem with your being part of his congregation. You have a choice: either you tell him that you are gay or you do not. It is up to you. But my advice is to get out of the order that you are in—and live life to the full."

Sebastian described the worst experience of his life as a time of "deep betrayal" by the Roman Catholic Church, an institution he had served faithfully since childhood, from altar server to priesthood. Yet growing up as an innocent country boy, Sebastian had discerned he was different from others, even though he had neither the language nor the understanding to articulate or make sense of the feelings inside him. This slow self-awakening was paralleled by an equally strong conviction that he should become a priest. He felt called, in particular, to help the poor and disadvantaged, a vocation that seemed somehow to connect with the sense of poverty, displacement and anxiety he felt about his own emerging sexuality. In the close-knit rural community, where romantic attachments spawned village gossip, Sebastian was spared cross-examination and congratulated on the sacrifices he was making. "There's no doubt priesthood gave me the opportunity to grow into my sexuality without people asking too many questions about why I didn't have girlfriends," he explained. "It was therefore a chance to become *me*. I tried to bury my sexuality and focus on my priestly vocation. On reflection, the motives for training to be a priest weren't entirely pure."

For Sebastian, priesthood became both a mask and a safety net. In the security of the training house, he became slightly more at ease with himself. But it was soon evident that it was not only his spirituality that was under formation. As Sebastian struggled to come to terms with homosexual feelings that showed no signs of abating, he began to hate himself and to loathe the path he had chosen. During many long months of loneliness and confusion, one book in particular brought comfort—Henri Nouwen's *Compassion*.[1] The paperback became the most dog-eared in his collection as he read and reread reassuring words about people being worthy of God's love no matter who they were or what they were going through. "That book kept me sane," said Sebastian. "I think homosexuality was a wound I didn't want anybody to see. I wanted the cloth still to be covering it. My anxiety was that if anybody saw that wound, they would not have tried to heal or love it. They might have attempted to deepen the hurt. Reading Nouwen's book gave me hope that I could be me and that I was worth something when all else around me was saying that I wasn't because I had these gay feelings. On reflection I am not sure that I would have continued without Nouwen's voice and support in his books."

A very good soccer player, Sebastian said there was nothing about his outer behavior that suggested he was gay. There was a "boy's club" culture in the seminary and Sebastian felt part of it. But internally he was less confident and needed guidance. Even though he was training for the priesthood in the liberated 1980s, sexuality made no appearance whatsoever on the curriculum. While he sensed two of the priests who taught him would have been sympathetic to his dilemma had he decided to share it, others appeared less approachable. Sebastian explained, "I think there was a rampant homophobia. Two priests who suspected I was gay were very hostile toward me. One even accused me of having an affair with another student. But while we loved each other as friends, we never had a sexual relationship. It was scary because these priests had power and could prevent you from becoming a priest because of your homosexuality. If I had disclosed to them that I had been gay, I do not think I would have been ordained. Homophobic people do not think rationally. They would not have believed for a second that any gay student could possibly be celibate, as I was. All the internalized anxieties of the priests in charge were probably being played out in the power they had over us."

Sebastian's reading of the situation is clearly borne out by the work of John Monbourquette, OMI, on the shadow side of person- alities and institutions. Monbourquette, a psychologist and priest, argues that an institution which cannot recognize its shadow will gradually begin to "deviate from its goals." Yet, by becoming so in- trigued by its shadow, it can end up promoting the very thing it is seeking to avoid. Monbourquette cites the case of two directors of a house of priestly formation who became "extremely preoccupied" with detecting the slightest signs of homosexuality and alcoholism among seminarians. An innocent gesture, such as tapping a friend on the shoulder, was interpreted as a sign of homosexuality. As a result, every member of the institution became obsessed with weeding out potential homosexuals and heavy drinkers. Seminarians even began to spy on one another, looking for the slightest indications. The shadows of the two directors finally poisoned the minds of the entire community and, instead of encouraging spiritual values, the formation house remained fixated on tracking down homosexuality and alcoholism.[2]

Sebastian was ordained at twenty-nine. The early years of priesthood lived up to expectations. He relished the work and felt he was making a difference to people's lives. While he acknowledges that there was "not a great deal of traditional piety" in his style of ministry, he believes it was built on a foundation of natural compassion and humanity. "It was about a living faith born out of suffering, reconciling who and what I was with a society and a church that did not want me to be me," he said.

Sebastian's study of Scripture led him to view the gospels as documents of love and inclusion, so he was prepared to take considerable risks in how he related to the congregation. At the beginning of every Mass, he would make sure those often excluded by church teachings were included: "You are very welcome here if you are gay and lesbian. If you are divorced, you are welcome. If you have had an abortion, you are welcome." In his homilies, whether in the parish or elsewhere on retreat, Sebastian did not flinch from addressing issues of racism, homophobia, or sexuality. He moved people—and challenged them. But while his words always went down well with most of those listening, they did not impress the authorities, who, like detectives hunting a wanted man, decided to act on a tip-off. Sebastian was suddenly banned from preaching in a diocese where he had given a retreat, while his provincial set about dispatching note-takers to the priest's own church on Sundays so they could record his words and report back.

Then, one morning, Sebastian was summoned to a meeting with the provincial. He was told to leave and work in the foreign missions. "The more I thought about it, the more I realized he wanted to get rid of me," Sebastian told me. "He wanted me outside. But I had not long been ordained and didn't think I was ready to go to abroad. That was something I wanted to do in the future. The provincial was very angry. He said he was concerned about some of my homilies, especially about my interest in people with HIV and AIDS and associating Jesus with their plight. He felt I had psychological issues. That's when he said, 'I think you're mad,' and sent me off for tests. I was not prepared to stay after that. I felt deeply, deeply betrayed and hurt. My dignity and humanity had been severely damaged."

Sebastian said he quit the priesthood, effectively because of his provincial's homophobia. He received a token amount of money but no real support to begin a new life. "It is the most hurtful thing that has happened to me," he disclosed. "In one sense it really destroyed my relationship with the institutional church—but not my relationship with God or my spirituality, which have been deepened and strengthened. However, I no longer practice any formal religion. I do not want to be part of the church while the provincial and others like him are perpetuating homophobia, and the church in Rome is issuing encyclicals that lack compassion and the gospel values of love. Through the humiliation, the hurt and the rejection, it has been a Passion-like experience. I think gay men can easily identify with the broken, wounded, hanging, bloody body of Christ on the cross. It's a real lived experience. And I think gay people are attracted to priesthood precisely because they can identify with that suffering Christ."

Sebastian has since become a successful therapist supporting members of disadvantaged communities. He reasons that he is more effective and compassionate in his work because of the hurts he has experienced as a gay person. His colleagues know he is gay but regard him as a whole person, viewing his sexuality as part of that completeness. Some might have had their prejudices softened by the sight of the human face of homosexuality among them. The institutional church, he feels, needs to show that face, loving after the pattern of Christ rather than isolating or demonizing those who are already marginalized by the world at large.

For several years now, Sebastian has been in a committed relationship with a fellow Catholic with whom he has set up home on the edge of a city in the United Kingdom. His partner, Dominic, is a former seminarian who now works in mental health. Dominic's journey has presented psychological problems of its own. As a teenager, he was abused by a member of his own parish congregation over a five-year period. The man, who was then in his mid-fifties, is now an elderly figure, still sitting in the front pew of the same church every Sunday. Following complaints of abuse against other youngsters, he was cautioned by police and placed on the sex offenders' register. But Dominic never made a formal complaint himself and, until now, has not spoken publicly about his own experiences.

At the height of the abuse, the man would regularly attend confession and insist that Dominic accompany him. "I was under his influence big time," Dominic told me. "I felt myself being drawn in but I was afraid to walk away." The man's possessiveness prevented the teenager from socializing with others. He would become jealous if Dominic met other friends so, for many years, they operated secretly as a couple. With its forty-year age difference, the friendship caused tensions within Dominic's immediate family and questions were raised in the parish. But Dominic dismissed the rumors and denied suggestions of abuse. "I think I lost a certain amount of my childhood," he said. "I really didn't know who I was. Fear was the fundamental factor in the control. I did not know what would happen if I split from this man. On many occasions he threatened suicide and that disabled me. In the end I decided to split from him. I accepted the consequences would have to be his not mine."

After extricating himself from this web of manipulation, Dominic found himself questioning his own sexuality. But he was confused and afraid. Family homophobia forced him into silence and further denial. Convinced he would be rejected if the truth were known, he put on the masks and became engaged to "a beautiful girl." Throughout the courtship, however, he doubted his heterosexuality and concluded that the relationship with her was dishonest. After seven months, he broke off the engagement, knowing how devastated the young woman would be. After the experience of abuse, Dominic wanted to be close to someone else. But all along he was evading reality, yet always too afraid to tell his girlfriend he was gay. "I was masking myself to do something that others did—

get married and have children," he told me. "I thought it was the norm, too, but it was only during this period that I realized that this norm wasn't a norm for me. When I eventually lifted the disguise and revealed to myself who I was, I began to find my own freedom. The anxieties disappeared and I was able to get in touch with my real emotions and feelings. At last I could be true to my self."

Dominic, then a tradesman, met Sebastian when he came to say mass at his parish church. He immediately felt a connection with him, drawn to his kindness, gentleness and generosity. They became good pals and, impressed by Sebastian's sense of vocation, Dominic decided to re-take the necessary exams so he, too, could go off to a seminary and become a priest. He joined a similar religious congregation, but eventually the two men lost touch with each other. Within the cloisters, however, Dominic continued to question his sexual identity, all the while astonished by the number of "gay and spiritual men" that seemed to exist in the priesthood. Many of his fellow students were homosexual. Most have subsequently left, he pointed out, and become openly gay. Training for the religious life was a time of self-discovery and bewilderment for Dominic, unveiling a breadth of reality he could never have previously imagined. He, too, felt supported by Nouwen's writings, especially *Life of the Beloved*.[3] "That book kept me going," he said. "Other people might not have accepted me for who I was but Nouwen's words persuaded me of the companionship of Christ's love for me as a human being who wanted to integrate my love for another. I felt I could still be beloved if I accepted the inner pain of my own sexuality."

He remained in the seminary for seven long years. The atmosphere became increasingly oppressive, almost closing in on him. There was always the blunt scent of denial as many gay students lived in fear of being found out. Too afraid even to mention the subject openly, they shouldered their sexuality as a constant burden. Dominic told me that he thought there had been a lack of integrity about the priesthood training—yet it had been that very hypocrisy that had eventually led him to acknowledge his homosexuality, at least to himself. "Students were not able to name this fundamental aspect of themselves for fear of wondering whether they would still be there the next day or the next week," he said. "It created great psychological damage to students because they could never be true to themselves. At the same time, I lost count at the number of retreat addresses when we were told by a priest that we should emulate the expression 'To thine own self be true.'"

Seminary life became unbearable. Dominic was on the point of departure when, fortuitously, he met up again with Sebastian, who had already left the priesthood. Dominic said he was never happier than on the night the two of them decided to form a relationship. Like any couple, of course, they have experienced difficulties but they believe their relationship has made them "more whole individuals." Dominic explained, "I don't believe I could do half as good the work I am doing in mental health today without my relationship with Sebastian. Now everybody knows who I am—that I am gay. I have no need to hide. There is no hypocrisy in the organization I work for. There are no masks, no walls being covered. Everybody knows everybody for what and who they are. This was the freedom I had been searching for. I certainly would not have found that had I been living a lie in the priesthood."

The couple feel unable to belong to a church community because they know they would not be accepted openly as partners. In view of the church's teaching about gay relationships, they were certain they would be stigmatized. But neither did they want to be ostentatious about their sexuality and cause further resentment. Christ came to bring love, freedom, and respect for each individual, Dominic pointed out, but the institutional church "breaks that down, instilling pain and hurt within itself because it does not accept that gay couples can offer life to others." Sebastian, meanwhile, mourned the fact that he could no longer say Mass but he had come to view people as sacraments. Indeed, his whole life had taken on a sacramental quality. "Hopefully I am bringing the presence of Jesus to the way I relate to people," he said. "They can see my love for Dominic and also see Christ in that love. I think our relationship is a physical sign of Christ here present. That is the understanding I have of faith in my life now. I am not prepared to open myself up to any more hurt."

Like many gay and lesbian people, Sebastian and Dominic feel they have come to understand love and pain as being intrinsically linked. The ultimate sign of a person's love is the figure of Jesus on the cross. The wound of homosexuality is not unrelated to Christ's presence in the Passion. Through suffering, rejection and pain, however, people grow, change and are transformed. The presence of a visible gay community within the church might enrich a congregation's understanding of Christ's passion, they suggested. Gay people have much to teach others about the broken body of Christ. The gay community, as a sacrament itself, could become "a powerful sign of the broken Christ which can change, grow and forgive." The suffering of gay and lesbian people has the potential to create a depth of understanding and compassion which straight people could learn from.

"I couldn't go back to the depressed state I was in—the loneliness, the struggle, the hypocrisy, knowing that I was living a lie," Dominic explained. "The only other option for me was to lift that mask, be true to myself and move. I hope some day I can be accepted in the Catholic Church. I would love to be able to sit in Mass and feel comfortable, knowing others are not judging me."

For Sebastian, however, going back to priesthood "would be like death" because "where I am now is life. It is full of faith and I am living the Gospel the way I believe it should be lived. I want the hierarchical church to tell me that it respects who I am and who Dominic is—that it respects us as a couple. Then we might be able to be welcomed in. But I am not going in by any back doors."

In their brightly decorated terraced house, adorned with framed photographs of a couple very solidly committed, Dominic and Sebastian said they felt more "confident and creative" for having taken the risk to allow another to love them. Dominic insisted he did not choose to be gay: "It chose me," he said, adding that homosexuality, rather than the priesthood, was perhaps his true vocation. A decade ago, he had fully expected to be living the life of a priest. "But it hasn't worked out the way I anticipated because God has been in the midst of it all. That is a blessing in disguise for me."

Sebastian described his homosexuality as "a beautiful gift, about who I am as a person, inseparable from my spirituality and my belief that God loves me for who and what I am." He said he valued his sexuality as divinely ordained because it provided him with the strength and courage to face ordeals and come through them, emerging as a more integrated, positive and happy individual. He recalled how, after he had left the priesthood, a close member of his family had died suddenly. At the funeral, Sebastian learned that the relative had always been worried that he would never find someone to love him. Sebastian's subsequent relationship with Dominic seemed to him like a blessing from heaven.

"I am glad the mask has finally gone," said Sebastian. "It was an awful pressure to try to hide it all inside and pretend to be someone I wasn't. I think I would have been mentally unwell if I hadn't taken the mask off at some point. I would have ended up in some form of serious depression. Then I really would have needed therapy. I have since learned what love is. I do not think I would have done so in the priesthood. There wasn't a lot of love there. I would have been living a very dark, unhappy, repressed existence as a priest in denial. I do not think I would have become so fully human and so fully alive in the way that Christ intended if I had not accepted the truth about myself and experienced the unconditional love of Dominic. I would not be the same person without him."

seven

Ages of Mystery

"If I became ill and couldn't be looked after in my own home, I hope I'd find a nursing home which would accept, understand and care for me as an older gay man."

The Reverend Bill Kirkpatrick is an Anglican priest in his late seventies. Through his pastoral ministry and spiritual books, he has helped many "go forth" on their spiritual journeys. During his life, Bill has had two long relationships, but both partners have died. "Life flows on and that is good," declared Bill on the day he had been given the all-clear after a series of hospital tests and several anxious weeks. "But I am always wondering what might become of me and how I might end my days. I know a gay priest who suffered a stroke and is now in a nursing home. He feels like an outcast because he is not being accepted by the staff for the person he is. It's probably a cause of his depressions."

Bill told me that, during his lifetime, he had seen vast changes in attitudes to homosexuality. "If I had my time over again I would still be a priest," he said, "but I would come out earlier and be more radical. I still feel I was guided toward my ministry to those on the margins. Only God can assess whether it has been of any use. What I have learned is that love and hope are the two essentials—a love that is as broad as it can be."

Growing up in Calgary, Canada, Bill always sensed he was different. He was in his late teens when it dawned he was gay but, like many men of his generation, he was frightened of talking about such matters openly. It was while he was working as a psychiatric nurse in Britain that he was forced to confront the reality. One day on his rounds a "highly psychotic" patient, who had clearly intuited his sexuality, challenged him to own it publicly. At the time they were taking part in a ward team conference. Suddenly the woman looked directly at him and asked why he was afraid of being a homosexual. A dumbfounded Bill, who had never considered himself overtly gay, felt himself blushing as the patient continued her piercing prognosis. "She told me that I was as good as any heterosexual, so I should stop being afraid because it was all right," Bill recalled. "I was very embarrassed by what she was saying so openly and only later realized that she had been merely asking me why I was so fearful of *my self*. Perhaps she was projecting some of her own vulnerability onto my own. It was a reminder that we were both vulnerable to life and the sanctions of society."

It was a turning point in Bill's self-development. After that he felt more comfortable in the company of others. He was later ordained, ministering to drug addicts in London's East End, homeless young people in Soho and the capital's gay community. For many years, from his home in Earls Court, he ran a one-man listening service called Reaching Out. It was particularly intended for people with chemical and sexual addictions, as well as for those living with HIV and AIDS. Every day he would sit "with a pair of big ears" eager to listen to anyone who cared to turn up. He made himself available for people of all ages, especially those who found themselves on the edge of society because they had difficulty coping with its expectations. He felt that, if he could reach in to himself, he could reach out to others.

"It is for ministers or priests to decide whether or not it is appropriate to reveal their sexuality," he told me. "I believe there should be no forced outings. It's essentially about how far you're prepared to be vulnerable to help the person beside you. I have found that, by being able to share what I have gone through, I have been able to connect with the sacred center of the other person."

Bill has always believed that sexuality and spirituality are united to each other as part of God's gift of himself to his creation. But in his early years of ministry he did not espouse such confidence. He remembered going into a pub wearing his clerical collar. As he stood self-consciously in the corner, clasping a drink, two men asked whether he was real. Then they began opening up about themselves. One turned out to be a police officer, the other a soldier. They talked about how difficult it was for them to live as gay partners because it necessitated the secrecy of an undercover military operation.

Suddenly one of them asked Bill if he were gay. It was a moment of utter vulnerability, especially as he was in professional attire. Bill did his best to duck the question. But he knew that he was merely attempting to protect his true identity. When he arrived home, he related the incident to his partner, who lambasted him for not being honest. "You are a gay man in a long-term relationship with another man," he shouted. "You are a committed Christian and an ordained priest. How can you not be truthful when you are going to be working with lesbians and gay men? They will be your parish. Your open presence and honesty will say more than anything else. Be the truth of love's openness."

This was another kairos moment for Bill, who went on to become a spiritual friend to many gay men scarred by their encounters with religious bigots and fanatical fundamentalists. Some had begun to doubt that they were acceptable to God, fearing they might ultimately be abandoned into eternal darkness or flames. But Bill would always reassure them with the words "God does not know how to reject." As Bill increasingly accepted the whole of himself, he concluded that being a gay person was actually a blessing from the God who had created him, a mystery to be lived to the full. Many gay people, he pointed out, preferred to talk of an ultimate "mystery" rather than of "God" because the image of a divine male parent was a bitter reminder of the pain they had experienced when they had been rejected by their fathers or other parental figures. For Bill, God was not so much a judge as "an ultimate lover."

Bill's first partner, Jim, was agnostic. After twenty years together, they moved away from each other while Bill was preparing for priesthood. The institutional church was an anathema to Jim. A month after Bill was ordained deacon in 1968, Jim married. He and his wife later attended Bill's first celebration of the Eucharist, having baked a small loaf which Bill consecrated and distributed in place of wafers. But as Bill grew into the solitude of the priesthood, he felt bereft of the love of his younger years. "I missed Jim very much, even though I realized that, if you really love someone, you have to let them go," he commented.

"I experienced a great deal of loneliness during this period. It was like a bereavement. It is well known that many bereaved people look for a sexual partner, simply to be reaffirmed as a person. As a substitute I threw myself into my new work with vulnerable young people who, unbeknown by them, helped to heal, to a certain extent, the sense of loss I felt."

Jim and Bill remained soul friends until the day Jim died. Bill believes they continue to be connected spiritually. Their last time of earthly sharing was in June 2001 when Jim was dying of cancer at his home in Canada. It was Bill's birthday and, despite his failing health, Jim baked him a cake as he had done during the first year they had been together as partners. They sensed they might not see each other again in this life but they remained in touch on the telephone almost every day until Jim "floated into the greater mystery" a few months later.

Bill met his second partner, Richie, through a mutual friend, in 1971. This relationship too lasted twenty years. After working together at the London homeless hostel, Centerpoint, they co-founded Streetwise Youth in 1985. It was the first project of its kind in the United Kingdom to advise, support and counsel young men involved in the sex industry on the streets of central London. That same year, however, Richie was diagnosed HIV-positive. Over the next six years, Bill cared for him tenderly. He decided to share in the care of his partner's dying and, as a result, the relationship was "deepened, authenticated and enriched." Bill explained that, in the midst of a mutually shared pain of loss, there was a growing awareness that they had entered a particularly sacred period of their relationship. It was important for both of them that Bill stayed alongside Richie in the London Lighthouse, a care center for people with HIV/AIDS, as much as possible during his final months and days. Honoring their special bond, the medical team allowed Bill, as a former nurse, to assist in the caring process. At Richie's request, it was agreed that Bill could be present when decisions were being made about medication and treatments.

Richie did not make a living will but, as his family was supportive of the relationship, he made it clear that Bill should be his spokesperson. "I spent a great deal of time with Richie every day and eventually stayed the night, sharing thoughts on many topics including his dying, the funeral service arrangements and the afterlife," said Bill. "We were there in the truth and in the trust of each other's love. I was allowed to nurse him through to his last breath. I have never forgotten the pain of realizing Richie was leaving this dimension of life and moving into the mystery beyond. I quietly reassured him of my continuing love. I said it was all right for him to let go if he wished. There was a sense our love would bridge the gap of separation."

As Richie died, Bill "saw and felt something leave his body," probably his "essentialness," or his soul entering the greater soul of all creation. With a nurse, he took part in "the sacred act" of washing his body, then prepared Richie for his coffin, dressing him in chosen clothing and taking off the ring which he was asked to keep as a token of the couple's continuing love and friendship. Bill offered a eulogy at the funeral. It was not an easy day and the committal proved the most painful stage of the grieving process, as it seemed to affirm their physical disconnection.

Richie had requested a champagne celebration of his life back at his flat after the funeral. After welcoming Richie's family from the North, Bill went out to buy the bubbly. When he returned, only a letter remained. "Sorry we must go. We have train to catch for Liverpool," it said bluntly. Bill remembered how he had felt "totally abandoned" at that point. "I returned to my own flat and played Mozart's *Requiem* as loud as I dared. I became totally immersed in the music. I experienced a kind of numbness as I tried to find my way through a cloud of unknowing."

In the following days, Bill needed to talk about the relationship with friends. But not all of them understood the depth of his friendship and the impact of the death. "I would often find myself asking Richie questions, talking to pictures of him around the flat, as well as reading his letters and diaries. At times tears would suddenly well up inside me, especially when I opened a book I had been reading and found a note inside it from him, expressing his friendship and love for me, always signed with a sketch of a flower. I decided to plant a yellow rose, a symbol of liberation, in the garden we both enjoyed."

As Bill continued his ministry among those living with HIV and AIDS, he was pleased to discover that the men increasingly accepted him as a priest. This had enabled him to "evolve spiritually." There was a growing inner awareness that both his sexuality and spirituality were linked to every cell in his body. When patients asked him about his own sexuality, he could respond to "these brothers and sisters of mine" that God had blessed him with a gift. "This appeared to allow many to be liberated into the wholeness of who they were becoming before they died," he told me. "Many would be searching for God through their illness, wondering if they would be ultimately acceptable. They would share their fears and anxieties—'I'm gay. Will God accept me or will I go to hell, as one priest said I would?' Or—'I don't believe in the church, if it won't accept me. How can I accept it and its negative attitudes toward differing sexualities?' In the midst of their dying many sensed they were moving into the mystery of wholeness."

As gay people mature, says Bill, they will feel secure enough in themselves to become elders and models to younger members of their community, offering meaning and enrichment at times of confusion and loneliness. As Bill himself has matured, so has his spiritual understanding, giving him the courage to live the truth of his life with hope. He remains comfortable with his "continuing liberation" toward the wholeness of becoming (through the "spirituality of my imperfections" and his "falling short of the mark") the person he really is. Having been alongside so many vulnerable people, Bill says he is now flowing with the river of life into a greater unknown future. Death is certainly about loss and separation, but life itself is "full of little separations" preparing us for the ultimate. As he put it so spiritually, "We emerged into this world through the mystery of birth, to live fully the mystery of our lives until we journey forward into a greater mystery."

eight

Hunted

Ever since he played a messenger in an outdoor production of *Macbeth,* performed around the school cricket pavilion, Daniel felt lured by the smell of the greasepaint. He had no difficulty learning lines, understood the dynamics of plot and could conjure up a host of accents to entertain his classmates. But as he fantasized about becoming a great actor on the London stage, he started to become aware of an identity that was much closer to home, a role for which he would receive little public acclamation. What alarmed him more was that fellow pupils seemed to sense he was gay as well. At a time when they too were starting to explore their sexuality, Daniel fell prey to their own projections, intimidated by the very friends who had once formed the audiences for his impromptu impersonations. Every day he found himself subjected to insults, humiliation and "relentless psychological torture."

Driving past the British school where it all happened, Daniel shuddered. It was a route he tried his best to avoid. He stopped the car and pointed toward the large sandstone chapel. "That's where I used to pray every morning for the bullying to stop, only to go into a class ten minutes later to find it flaring up all over again," he recalled. "I lived my entire lower- and upper-fifth years of school in trepidation but, because the bullying was directed at my perceived sexuality, I was too frightened to tell my parents or the staff.

"I remember a teacher even colluding with the banter when one of the pupils had a dig at me through a witticism. The master smirked at the joke. But he should have challenged it. We had been asked to broaden our reading so I had gone into a small library in the English department and innocently selected G. K. Chesterton's *A Man Called Thursday*. A fellow pupil, observing my choice, rushed out to the others, declaring, 'Trust Daniel to pick a book with *man* in the title.' I raised some of these issues with another member of staff but he simply responded by asking if I thought it might be my fault."

Daniel explained that each week, as elaborate rumors circulated around heavily polished corridors, he became increasingly unpopular and the daily target of humiliating taunts. On one occasion, he became suspicious of a piece of paper being passed round the class. When it eventually reached his desk, Daniel felt his stomach churning and heartbeat racing as he realized the pupils were conducting a poll to find out if anybody liked *him*. On the sheet lay twenty-six stark "no's" and two abstentions. He also noticed that a "yes" had been scrawled out.

Sometimes he would just sit in a cloakroom, away from everyone, holding his head in his hands. But even that did not always provide the refuge he desperately sought. One day he looked up and found incriminatory words about him daubed across the walls. On another occasion, when he came top in an exam, he was picked up, carried unceremoniously around the school and thrown onto the hard shower-room floor. He could still feel that sudden encounter with concrete. Later, he heard the chief adversary telling the others, "There's nothing wrong with doing well in an exam, except when it's *him*."

The bullying continued after classes too. Passing a bus-stop where he had often been verbally (and sometimes physically) accosted, Daniel admitted that, even to this day, he grew distinctly uneasy when approaching a menacing group of youths in the street. "I expect them to start making kissing noises with their lips or to sneer at me with some gay jibe," he said. "I could have understood it if I had been meeting a boyfriend after school but I was only vaguely aware of my emotions and I certainly hadn't had any intimate relationships. But the psychological bullying seemed to go on relentlessly."

Further along the road, Daniel spotted the parish church where, at the height of the persecutions, he had sometimes taken shelter from the torrent of abuse. He remembered identifying with the figure nailed to a large crucifix. He had looked up at Christ on the cross and felt embraced. "In my great loneliness and fear, I was able to connect with that pierced wooden body. My Christian faith seemed to grow out of those spiritual conversations. I think I would have had a more fragmented sense of self had I not rooted my identity in God from the outset."

Daniel said that, every night, he would write up what had happened to him in a journal. "But I used a special code so that, if anybody ever read it in the future, they would not realize the taunts were about my being gay," he explained. "I'm not sure I even knew what gay meant in those days, but the experience of being demeaned and ostracized for it seriously undermined my self-confidence."

Years later, the lyrics of the Bronski Beat song "Small Town Boy," reminded him of his teenage predicament:

Run away, turn away, run away, turn away, run away
Run away, turn away, run away, turn away, run away

Pushed around and kicked around
Always a lonely boy
You were the one
That they'd talk about around town
As they put you down

And as hard as they would try
They'd hurt to make you cry
But you never cried to them
Just to your soul
No you never cried to them
Just to your soul

He went on to recall how a group of horn-blowing hunters had once chased a deer through a local scenic area and into the sea. They had cheered as they watched the antlers of the struggling animal sinking beneath the water. "That was barbaric in the extreme," exclaimed Daniel, "but I think that I identified with that poor stag because it was an image of cruel pursuit, reminiscent of what I had gone through psychologically as a teenager."

Between the ages of 16 and 18, Daniel studied at another school where, to his amazement, he became popular, not least for his performances in its theatrical productions. He also discovered that at least twelve other students there were gay. Although the mutual recognition was only implicit, he nonetheless felt in safe company. When Daniel began work in a local office, the gay taunting resurfaced. Every lunchtime he would have to run the gauntlet of a row of manual workers who called out to him with a mocking effeminacy. He was always courteous and friendly, but never camp or exuberant. How did they know? He cringed as, day after day, they pursed their lips and made kissing noises that seemed to have come back to haunt him. It was as though he were marked for life by a taint that only other men could detect. But it was all based on assumption because Daniel was hardly out to himself. He said such smears had plagued him throughout his career. It could only be put down to his gentle, caring nature and a spiritual approach to life. He was different.

But Daniel thought his sensitivity had also enabled him to be more compassionate to others who suffered. He said he often felt closest to God when sitting beside the bedside of a sick or dying person when he could enter into their pain. Visiting friends on psychiatric wards came naturally to him, especially among patients with mental health problems who were themselves stigmatized.

Daniel wondered if his fantasy of becoming an actor might, at some level, have been associated with his low self-esteem. A standing ovation for a solo performance might have given a gay person a degree of affirmation to compensate for any lingering insecurities. Although Daniel later worked for a national company, it was not with a theatrical troupe. If being a gay man in the provinces had been difficult enough, surviving alone in a strange city was twice as daunting. Several of his older colleagues happened to be openly gay and immediately detected the new boy was too. Moreover, it gradually dawned that they were attracted to *him*. But because Daniel had still not really come to terms with his identity and was always in denial, he found the atmosphere stifling. As he watched others, not exactly parading, but more at ease with their sexuality, he felt he was looking at a wall of mirrors—and the reflection disturbed him.

"I felt very threatened and very frightened by it," he said. "After all the gay insults I had absorbed at school, I suddenly found myself in an environment which was gay-friendly, yet I couldn't handle it. Looking back, I realize I didn't have the courage to come out to myself because I had associated homosexuality with the humiliation I had experienced at school. It had prevented me from owning who I was. Then the projection set in. I started telling friends that I was working with a gay crowd and didn't feel at home. But the truth was, in one sense, I could not have been *more* at home. I was repelled by the very thing I was."

Being gay continued to take its toll on him psychologically. "You have no idea how people will react to the truth of who you are, so you invent girlfriends, pretend to be macho and devise scenarios to put people off the scent. That's where the acting comes in," he smiled. "I think that fundamentally it's about minimizing the sense of rejection people like me feel so acutely. You live constantly under the threat of another insinuation. Although you would like to be open and relaxed about who you are, you can never guarantee the reaction of the people you're with, if they don't already know or haven't yet guessed. At the same time, you live in fear of any close interrogation of your personal life. You protect your deepest self at all costs because you don't want to be hurt any more. Straight people don't seem to live like that."

Once in Granada, watching the Holy Week processions curving through the medieval Spanish city, Daniel was moved to tears because he could enter into Christ's suffering with a particular understanding. It took him back to his schooldays. Being gay had nonetheless brought him closer to Christ, even if it had distanced him from the institutions that acted in Christ's name. He received the sacrament of Holy Communion as often as he could but did not feel he *belonged* to any congregation. He had "no doubt," however, that God had created him, "for whatever reason," to be a gay man in the world, and he had a profound sense of calling.

"I don't think I can pretend that the wounds are not there, any more than the risen Christ could hide the holes in his body from the apostle Thomas," Daniel admitted. "In fact, it was the wounds in Christ that made him believable to Thomas. But wounds can only become glorious when their origins are acknowledged and when their pain enables you to care for others with greater compassion. And that includes those who have wounded you, which is not always easy.

"Years after I had been bullied at school, I came face to face with one of the perpetrators in a wine bar. At first I tried to avoid eye contact but then he spoke, 'I was at school with you, wasn't I? We gave you a hard time, didn't we?' I nodded and he turned his head. It was clear he did not wish to continue the conversation. Inwardly I was sad because, in that moment of brief reconnection, I wanted more to hug him than retaliate—just to be accepted by him again."

nine

Masks of Compassion

"I regard myself as a friend to God's outcast children," said Michael Harank as we sat chatting in the Bay area of San Francisco. "It's a circle of friendship that extends to people in the gay community, the homeless, drug abusers, the mentally and physically ill and the dying."

Michael was born into a working-class family of six children of French-Canadian and Hungarian heritage in the city of Lynn, Massachusetts, which was the women's shoe factory capital in the world at the turn of the twentieth century. He attended Catholic schools for most of his education, acquiring a bachelor's degree in religious studies from the College of the Holy Cross in 1976, the first in three generations of Americans to receive a college education. He was awarded a nursing degree in 1987 after working at St. Rose's Home for the Incurably Ill with Cancer in New York City, a hospice for the poor founded by the Catholic convert Rose Hawthorne, the youngest daughter of the American writer Nathaniel Hawthorne.

For more than twenty years Michael has been part of the Catholic Worker movement. He lived with Dorothy Day in the last years of her life and carried the processional candle at her funeral in 1980. For many years, he ran a Catholic Worker house of hospitality in Oakland, California, for homeless people, and those living and dying with HIV/AIDS.

Michael convened the first gathering/retreat of Lesbian, Gay, Bisexual and Transgender Catholic Workers in 1996. It was attended by people from thirteen states and three countries. He is currently active in his parish ministry with the LGBT Catholic group and with Soulforce, an interdenominational movement addressing "the legacy of spiritual violence against queer people" in the various Christian denominations. Michael has been arrested for non-violent civil disobedience more than twenty times in protest against war, nuclear weapons, nuclear power, farm worker rights, and gay rights. He was a religious conscientious objector during the Vietnam War.

Aged fifty, he now works at a public hospital for the poor and uninsured as the director of its HIV/Hepatitis C clinic. Hepatitis C is now a leading cause of death for people with HIV in the United States and currently affects four million people.

As a registered nurse and a gay man, Michael was clearly the one to examine the "wound of homosexuality," of which denial, fear and alienation form three interconnected, yet distinguishable, components. He told me that he believed it arose out of a reluctance on the part of some gay people to accept their sexuality as a gift. "When such a wound bleeds a lot without attention being paid to it, the person ends up losing a lot of blood and a lot of life. That part of a person's identity was not fed by the great symbol of life which is blood. It atrophies, constricts and eventually causes death and the destruction of the body."

When gay people fail to pay attention to the wound or pretend it doesn't exist, they operate at a level of denial that can result in behavioral patterns that are psychologically harmful. As some of the conversations in this book illustrate, the most common trait is a natural compulsion to disguise, a technique homosexuals perfect almost unthinkingly as the years of suppression continue. On a human level, of course, denial and disguise each have their place in the spectrum of human meaning. But, according to Michael, denial is prone to become an essential coping mechanism when gay people are not ready to deal with the darker or shadow side of their personalities. Disguise, therefore, becomes the means through which gay people communicate. "This can result in colorful and creative behavior as, like costumed actors, they manifest a certain theatricality as a means of touching the truth of their God-given humanity," said Michael. As a keen observer of gay culture once observed, "Art is spirituality in drag." But, conversely, disguise can also "breed a cesspool of secrecy which becomes a stagnant pond instead of turning into the waters of creativity." Gay priests in particular tend to operate at the level of camouflage. Instead of appreciating their sexuality as a gift, they attempt to drown, he explained. This created suffering not only for those clergy themselves, but also for those they served.

He went on, "Gay people use denial to run away from what can be a great stirring water of the Holy Spirit. For gay priests this terrible struggle can get expressed in unhealthy relationships with themselves and with others. They are unable to break out of the vicious circle of secrecy and suspicion. Denial and disguise eventually create a kind of hell for them and the people around them." The film *Priest* illustrates this point.[1] In one scene, the main character—a Catholic priest who is gay—is seen removing his clerical collar, putting on a leather jacket and leaving his Merseyside rectory for a gay bar in Liverpool. There is a sense that one identity is being supplanted by another: the priest takes off his clerical disguise and puts on "gay attire" so he will feel part of a homosexual context. When he gets back from the parish, the camera homes in on his taking off the jacket and replacing it with clerical attire, his double identity encapsulated in a few slick frames. For Michael, the scene is a classic example of "the kind of spiritual schizophrenia" that results from a gay person not being able to welcome an essential part of his humanity—the gift of sexuality. If a gay man is unable to accept "that primary reality" in which all creation participates, he becomes dissociated and schizoid. But, if he can, he becomes "more deeply human and more deeply divine."

"My experience of gay priests, both diocesan and religious, is that there is no place of sanctuary for them within their communities to bring that gift to each other because there is such a terrible accumulation of guilt, repression, secrecy and suspicion around the issue of sexuality," said Michael. "They carry it around with them like a bag of bones. The great image of Ezekiel, creating this very living figure out of those bones, does not find expression in their lives."

Straight people did not have to conceal their gift of sexuality. But Michael conceded that gay men and lesbians sometimes had little option but to hide, for fear of rejection and being ostracized. The blessing of sexuality, therefore, became a cross and a wound. Unlike the Native American communities that had rituals for calling out the various gifts in the community at a very young age, the Catholic Church had never developed any kind of rite or sacred space to do that. When a community failed to call out such a gift, gay people were in danger of developing a Dr. Jekyll/Mr. Hyde mentality. Their emotional life often became skewed and afflicted. "They run in fright or prepare to attack as animals do when they are being pursued by a perceived enemy," said Michael. "Isn't that what happened with the character in the film *Priest* until he could run no more?"

Michael thought, nonetheless, that almost every culture utilized the mask as a way of communicating "a certain lived emotion of our lives." The way in which Indonesian or Native American masks functioned in their communities through music and dance illustrated how masks could allow the creative expression of the emotions they represented. Raw energy was channeled into a recognizable face through which a particular story could be shared with the community. Ultimately life was about being able to share one's story as part of the collective story of suffering, redemption and salvation, made meaningful through the power of love.

"I feel gay priests have been facing the community wearing only the masks of these negative emotions—of fear, suspicion, anxiety, secrecy and shame. I think we are coming to a time when we are just beginning to be able to express creative, healthy and integrated masks that sexuality can foster within a community. We are about to paint new masks of compassion and solidarity, connecting the suffering of gay people with others who are marginalized and ostracized. We should be using masks, as so many tribal rituals do, to reveal the essence of who we are as God's children—his hands and feet and heart, and eyes in this world."

Michael believed this form of mask-wearing could create an environment where justice, reconciliation, co-operation, and compassion could co-exist, whereas masks of denial and disguise were not helpful in establishing such unity. Jesus' deepest prayer had been the prayer of unity: "that they might be one." A gay man could only "become one" if he brought all of himself to the table or altar of the Eucharist," where the drama of all our lives are enacted." The masks of sexuality in the church and among gay priests in particular had been "dark, negative and menacing." New masks were needed to integrate the gift of sexuality in such a way that all people were liberated to be friends with one another in a way that Jesus called his disciples to be friends to each other.

Much theological language around sexuality had become so spiritualized and out-of-the-body that it was simply another way of avoiding the reality of God's creating people as sexual beings: The erotic, creative energy within each of us was denied, and, often out of self-disgust, the unrevealing and toxic masks went on. Moreover, the very theological language used by the Vatican in relation to homosexuality revealed "a deep measure of violent self-hate and self-loathing" projected onto the gay community.

"But of course we will always wear masks," he added. "Even in the accounts of the resurrection, there is a mask-like quality in Jesus' presence in the new life. The disciples recognize that. Even when people have begun to integrate their sexuality into their lives, enabling them to acknowledge their humanity and its purpose, they still wear masks but they are masks of a different way of being—one that reveals the deepest human and spiritual truths about being made in the 'image and likeness of God.'

"A person who is hidden in a dark closet, whether a victim of abuse or a victim of secrecy or shame or a victim of homophobia, has a very different face from the one who has come out of the closet into the light. But it is always a light that reveals and shadows at the same time. The light of the resurrected body of Christ is not the shadow light of humiliation but the luminous light of humility—the one virtue that opens the doors to all the other virtues necessary for the fullness of a spiritual-sexual life of joy and gratitude."

ten

Terminal Loneliness

"The more I can own my gay self, both privately and in therapy," Father Nathan told me, "the more it becomes possible for me to relate more meaningfully to others."

Like many homosexual priests in the Roman Catholic Church, Father Nathan is keenly aware of the conflicts that could exist between his public role in the parish and his private identity as a gay man. Many years of psychotherapy have helped heal the inner dichotomies. As a priest, he occupies a role and plays a variety of parts for the people around him. For him, the priesthood is about being all things to all people, a culture in which he has had to learn to allow some dimensions of his personality to come to the fore and others to recede, depending on the situation. "Within that context, it's very easy for the whole of your sexual life to be in disguise," he observed.

Pouring Earl Grey tea in the study of his modern and tastefully furnished rectory, in a corner of the United Kingdom he asked me not to disclose, Nathan admitted that coping with so much secrecy over the years had left him in a state of "terminal loneliness." He said he believed concealment could lead to a serious personality malfunction. If a person's sexuality were not owned, the multiple parts could not function in harmony and this could result in psychological dissonance. But when all facets of the personality could be held together consciously and healthily, enrichment was possible. "Wholeness is the key," he explained. "A person is not a two-dimensional being but a rich and complex individual whose various components need to be brought into the conscious mind and worked with in a creative way. But in the case of gay priests this cannot happen easily because the church fails to address the issue of homosexuality. By necessity, it is cloaked in secrecy. But as I become more self-aware, through the process of ageing and through the process of engaging in long term psychotherapy, less and less of me is concealed to myself."

For nine years Nathan lived in "a deep and loving" relationship with another priest. The warmth of this friendship and its importance to Nathan were tacitly understood both by his bishop and those who knew the couple. Nathan and Jason did not feel they were deceiving other people, even though there was little explicit acknowledgement. Within the ecclesiastical world, love between priests was encouraged and not frowned on, said Nathan, a bonding which might be talked about in terms of "mutual support." After all, fraternity had always been an integral facet of priesthood. "The relationship did not really throw me into confusion at all. It felt very peaceful and lasted very well. I did not feel destabilized. I felt as though I had come home."

But when Jason decided to leave both the relationship and the priesthood, Nathan was devastated. An enclosed life of love and belonging ended abruptly, with all the force of a sudden bereavement. "I remember sitting in the lounge and feeling a radical aloneness," he said. "I imagine it's what an abandoned infant feels. The very state of isolation was life-threatening. I think I would have died there and then had I not been in therapy and had I not sufficiently internalized my own therapist. I found enough energy within me to get to the telephone and ring her. I cannot imagine what might have happened had I not been engaged in that kind of process. It felt as if there were no one else in the world to turn to. The only thing I had to hang on to was the memory of the people I met in the course of my therapy and the therapist herself. The relationships I had in my therapy world were more three-dimensional, more accepting, more real and more genuine than those in the church."

Although he now lives alone, Nathan thinks all people need "someone to rest in." Hyperactivity, the trait of many gay priests, becomes an avoidance of loneliness and isolation, a means of making connections with people which at times can be creative, productive and helpful. But they are often a substitute for a shared intimacy, a compensation, "a way of coping."

Born and bred a Catholic, Nathan grew up with an awareness of his orientation but without the linguistic skills to articulate his emerging emotions. He thought he was the only person in the world who felt as he did. People might have suspected he was homosexual, but there was certainly no communication about it from family, society, or the church. However, before Nathan's mother died, he decided to broach the subject with her for the first time. He was somewhat surprised to learn that she had gathered he was gay for a quarter of a century. "I asked why she had not said anything about it," said Nathan. "She replied that she did not think she could raise the matter. It was up to me. I think that was a failure in her parenting and a failure in the social preparation for her parenting. But I am not blaming her. She simply could not articulate it. She was as much a victim of the situation as I was."

One of the roles of a parent, Nathan suggested, was to help children understand themselves and provide interpretative keys for that experience. This had been denied him in the area of sexuality and had, to some extent, impeded the formation of his personality. Recalling a radio program about an English mother who had adopted a young girl from China, Nathan said that, as he had listened to that broadcast, he had been impressed by the woman's attitude toward parenting. She had become concerned that her adopted daughter never cried and had concluded that this was the consequence of the girl's experience in an orphanage. There the child must have cried a lot but no one had ever come over to pick her up and cuddle her. So the mother decided she would have to "model" the child into crying so she would know if the girl needed anything. "It is a great pity that gay people don't get that kind of modeling as children and are not encouraged to open up," said Nathan "They just have to find out later."

For Nathan, who felt called to be a priest from an early age, the seminary became a safe haven for a young man aware of his homosexual identity but lacking the vocabulary to share its implications with others. The priesthood subsequently provided safety and containment because Nathan did not have any models for his homosexuality. In offering a ready-made identity, the priesthood supplied the remedy. "It gave me a role that I still put on like a suit of clothes before work can begin," he said. "But I had to go looking for that suit because, in my innermost being, nothing had really been constructed. I had to find an external identity because the internal work had not been accomplished. I imagine gay people find their way into nursing, teaching and other forms of service for much the same reason. It is also a means of being generative and creative, of having children as it were, of helping others to mature and to grow. All those parenting characteristics find their home in being a priest."

Nathan said he had needed to discover contacts and influences outside the church in order to survive within it. It had been a case of "adolescence revisited." Just as in his youth there had been no positive language about homosexuality and no visible signs of its existence, so the priesthood itself mirrored those years. It was not that he was trying to recreate the church in his own image and likeness—because many other Catholics experienced the institution in much the same way. But the territory did feel familiar and had taken him back to his youth. The experience had scarred him psychologically and could not in any sense be viewed in a positive light. He owed a great deal to the church and had a great love for it. But there was "absolutely no getting away" from the damage it had caused as well.

Although Nathan was once ambitious, he said he would find it difficult these days to accept a prominent position in the Catholic Church. He speculated that one of the reasons why he had not been "invited into the center" might have been related to the fact that, in certain Catholic circles, he had been more vocal about his homosexuality than other priests. He saw himself hovering on the edge of the church and at times wondered why he remained a priest. His reasons for staying were not only related to having a sense of security but were also related to his love of the liturgy as well as "a certain bloody-mindedness about hanging on in there" and trying to work for something better.

He felt nothing constructive was emerging from the Vatican to help those with a homosexual orientation make sense of their lives in a creative way. "All the language is destructive and I feel very angry about this," he told me. The way in which the Vatican referred to gay people as morally disordered or inclined to intrinsically evil acts hardly provided a rich seedbed for healthy growth and maturity. They were "terrible phrases" to speak about anybody. "I would not want to say anything in their favor," he added.

Nathan said he felt particularly sad that the church had not provided a context within which he could think, explore, and develop as a gay man. The Catechism of the Catholic Church stated that gay people should not be discriminated against, so mixed messages were coming out of Rome. He said he tried to cling onto the positive statements but most of the time found the approach destructive. In reality, though, the church was much more of a "containing" institution than many might think. In Roman Catholicism, the principles were clearly established but much pastoral support moved around the guideline boundaries, especially in terms of the welfare of homosexuals and of divorced and remarried Catholics.

The priest explained how he had learned to be inventive and creative about the difficulties he faced every day. He drew strength from the *Exsultet*, which is sung at the Easter Vigil Mass: "O happy fault. O necessary sin of Adam which gained for us so great a redeemer." He also found encouragement in M. Scott Peck's book *The Road Less Traveled*, which opened with the words "Life is difficult." Nathan elaborated, "I accept Scott Peck's thesis that, in as much as we engage positively with the difficulties which confront us, we grow mentally and spiritually healthy. But in as much as we avoid the problems, we become less mentally and spiritually alive. Gay people and gay priests are confronted with a particular set of great difficulties. In as much as they can engage with those difficulties, they can arrive at a place of real spiritual and mental health. But as much as they avoid them, they can find themselves in a state of great desperation and disaster."

There was no doubting the fact that, for many people, homosexuality was a painful place to be in, yet the creative gifts homosexual people had brought to the church and to the world at large down the centuries were unquestionable. In a sexualized culture where gay people were no longer silenced, many were finding the confidence to speak from their own perspectives. This was challenging the Catholic Church, but there was a danger that the issue was becoming focused on gay people. "I've rarely heard a bishop or a Catholic priest speaking enthusiastically about the church's teaching on contraception," he remarked. "That teaching is received in utter silence, so effectively it's not received at all. One of my concerns is that gay people are put under the spotlight because it's quite convenient to locate all the difficulties in them, whereas the reality is that there is much discomfort in the church around sexuality in general. Most young Catholics seem to have had sex before marriage and there is plenty of circumstantial evidence to suggest that quite a lot of Catholics use artificial means of birth control. So I think there is a real difficulty in the church about its teaching on sexuality. The gay issue is actually one aspect of a much broader reaction."

As a result, Catholics were taking more responsibility for their own decisions and, indeed, their own lives. Attitudes were different from those of half a century ago when every Catholic was supposed to be "a camp-follower." Individuals were now moving from a culture of dependency into situations where they laid claim to a much greater degree of autonomy, an independence of thought and behavior which attempted to engage with the world more critically than ever before. The stifling protection of Roman Catholicism's seamless robe was slowly being discarded by many Catholics.

Not that, in Nathan's eyes, the Church of England's grass was any more verdant. "The Jeffrey John affair was far more of a witch-hunt than you would be allowed to get away with in the context of the canon law of the Roman Catholic Church," he said. "There seems to me to be a logical inconsistency within Anglicanism. It appears to offer a wider context for discussion and moving on but in fact it is flawed because it has an internal incoherence. This makes it very difficult to subscribe to. I can never get my head around the idea that you can be in communion with people with entirely opposing views on very important matters like the ordination of women and the place of gay people in the church. The way in which pragmatism seems to give way to principle distresses me. That the Archbishop of Canterbury's overriding concern is to keep the communion together seems to be a betrayal of principle.

"I have thought about leaving the active ministry sometimes but that would not be the same as leaving the church. I've considered the alternatives, such as Anglicanism and Orthodoxy, but for me Roman Catholicism remains persuasive. It is my home. I won't be dispossessed of it. I am a valid part of it and not an invalid part of it. Show me a family where there are no tensions, rivalries, conflicts—or even power struggles."

eleven

The Wedding Veil

Mark is a middle-aged father of two who comes from an evangelical background in the South of England. Ordained an Anglican priest, he was highly regarded by his parishioners as a creative and caring pastor. But throughout his married life Mark hid his homosexuality from himself and his family. Then, almost overnight, his marriage broke up and he had to leave his parish. Eventually, he entered a relationship with another man.

As a young evangelical worshiper in England, he had been aware that homosexuality as an issue was never broached in his church, except through occasional judgments by fellow Christians who pronounced that all homosexuals would burn in hell. Even as a child, Mark knew that included him. "I didn't want to burn in hell so, at the age of eleven, I went into denial," he told me.

As someone with a healthy respect for Scripture, Mark said he could not recall how he had managed to reconcile the fundamentalist position on homosexuality with an awareness of his own nature. He began to reason that straight people viewed texts through straight lenses. In coming to terms with their sexuality, gay people went through a process of exchanging heterosexual lenses for homosexual ones. For example, Mark saw both beauty and innocence in the "gay love story" of David and Jonathan, even though his evangelical contemporaries would have interpreted the relationship differently. "I wanted to be a good evangelical," said Mark. "But, during my teenage years, I was trying to come to terms with these same-sex feelings. I was attempting to justify them, not to people in the church, but to myself and to God. I think I accepted that this was the way God had created me and I had learned that God never created anything bad."

As a boy, Mark sensed a calling to priesthood. He said he heard God's voice telling him he was to be ordained. It never deserted him, even when he left school and went into one of the caring professions. The homosexual feelings persisted too. In the end, he married and was later selected for ordination training at an evangelical theological college. One day, during a lecture on morality, he said he had listened to the best argument he had ever heard for gay love. The lecturer had said, "God is love, and where love is, there is God." Mark said he had suddenly realized it was perfectly possible for two men to love each other. When any person loved another, the beauty of God was evident in that love.

Mark was ordained in his early thirties. The night before he was ordained deacon, however, he slept with one of the other students, whom he knew to be gay. "Sleeping with this other guy, who was also being ordained the following day, might have been wrong but, as I reflected on it later, there was something right about it too. It was about being ordained *as a gay man*. But I never told my wife what happened that night." The couple went on to have children but, although he "tried to be a caring husband and father," he knew he was reaching a stage when the *real* him would have to break through the guise of an apparently happy marriage. He remembered preaching on a verse from St. John's Gospel—"I have come that they might have life and have it in abundance"—and knowing in his heart he was living a lie.

"My wife knew there was something wrong," he said. "We had got to the point where she insisted we went to see a counselor. She was so upset and so distressed. In spite of her being very intuitive, she never suspected I was gay. All my gay friends wondered how she did not guess. Gay people know gay people. Straight people think they know gay people, but actually they don't."

Mark described the relationship with his wife as having been a "positive, enriching and wholesome experience," although the day he came out to her had been the beginning of a process that had engineered the breakdown of a marriage and a family, a situation he profoundly regretted. His priestly ministry was suspended.

"At my lowest ebb, I crashed spectacularly," he told me. "I lost my family, the place where I lived and my job virtually. I had nowhere to live, so I'd rough it—even stay in the car. Although I'd been offered somebody's house, I felt so low I slept on the floor. I needed to look the darkness in the face and see it eye to eye. Only after that could I begin the process of my own recovery. The picture language of the psalms about abandonment, darkness and the questioning of where God was all presented themselves to me in the darkness. It was a personal crucifixion and I couldn't resurrect until I was truly dead. That is what it felt like."

He recalled the sense of rejection he had experienced when a heterosexual bishop had suggested it was wrong for him to be a homosexual. He had felt judged and, for a time, had wanted to abandon the church. Nonetheless, he said he was prepared to "carry on being broken because there is creative tension in that."

Mark has since been supporting other married men who are gay. Most had been in denial for years, he said, and had colluded with being straight to their family and friends. Only later had the real person in each of them begun to emerge. Many were tormented by feelings of guilt. But, having come out to their families, there had been healing and reconciliation. "I think it is more difficult discovering you are gay when you are married and have children because you don't have only yourself to think about," he explained. "You have a spouse whom you've committed yourself to, loved and had children with. All of those factors compound the real issue about being homosexual. It depends on a person's emotional make up as to whether married men come out. A lot secretly have sex with other men but don't identify themselves as being gay and remain in their marriage. People unsure of their sexual identity still need to belong to a family, and the family option is marriage and children."

He could identify with Gene Robinson, who had formerly been in a married relationship with a family. Those very people had greeted him on the day of his consecration. There had been a healing, forgiveness, acceptance and a moving on. "Bishop Robinson's personal journey is similar to my own," said Mark. "My wife now has a new partner and she has floated the possibility of getting married to him. The thought had crossed my mind whether it would be possible for me, as her ex-husband and as a priest, to conduct her re-marriage."

Time and again gay men and lesbians had sacrificed themselves in the so-called battle against fascist, heterosexual orthodoxy. When he had watched the television news and seen Gene Robinson being consecrated, he had found himself saying, "Well done mate." It had been "a very brave decision" on Gene Robinson's part to go ahead. He was not sure, however, that it was necessarily right for the Anglican Communion at the time.

Mark thought that, having accepted his own homosexual identity, he had become a more effective priest: "I think people, who know who they are, can be an incredible blessing to the church and, as long as they are not in denial, gay men and women are set free to experience the abundant life," he remarked. "It is about a sense of integrity. What I learned over and over again as an evangelical was that God wanted us to be the people he had created us to be. I think Jesus was an incredible person of integrity and, if we can follow in his footsteps to any degree, that is a blessing. Jesus said the truth sets you free and he spent time with the nameless people on the margins. I have experienced Jesus coming and meeting me as a nameless person and bringing me back into center-court to carry on the game.

"I regret the fact I wasn't able to own my sexuality earlier. But I don't know how I would have coped with it in relation to the church if I had been out and proud as a teenager. That would probably have ruled out any idea of ordination. I regret that I had to wait until my mid-forties to finally find the courage, strength and acceptance. Why did I have to wait for forty five years to be the person I've been since the day I was born? That is deep regret. I don't blame God, but I blame the church's mishandling of what the church has perceived to be truth, fed to me through the evangelical tradition.

"I spent most of my life pretending and covering up. Now I don't have to. I wouldn't change it for anything because, with a smile on my face, I can look at you and say *this is me*."

twelve

Noontide

Sunlight streamed into the lounge, catching his reflection in the window, as I walked up to the house in West London. He was sitting there alone in the front room, his face illuminated in the window glass. Jonathan had been a successful lawyer in the City. Now, at the age of forty, he was dying of AIDS. He told me that he had been HIV-positive since he was in his late twenties and had moved "from Gethsemane to Calvary." He then read me a prayer he had written:

> *We did not want it easy God*
> *But we did not think that it would be*
> *Quite this hard, quite this long or quite this lonely.*
> *So please in your love and at your will*
> *Grant us a cure.*

When Jonathan received his full AIDS diagnosis, he was lying in a hospital bed. As the news sank in, he felt "totally destroyed." He later found himself identifying with the words of the Trappist monk Thomas Merton: "True love and prayer are learned in that moment when prayer has become impossible and the heart has turned to stone." Jonathan looked toward me. "I've been there," he said. Then, movingly, he quoted the Canticle of Hezekiah, "In the noontide of my days I must depart."

The HIV/AIDS epidemic was first reported in June 1981. In 1983 the human immunodeficiency virus (HIV) was discovered to be the causative agent of AIDS. The year 1985 had seen the licensing of an antibody test to diagnose the presence of HIV infection, and in 1987 the licensing of AZT created the first specific anti-HIV therapy. AIDS, said Jonathan, presented an opportunity for everyone to face their humanity, mortality, and sexuality. It ought not to be viewed as a disease or "gay problem" but as an occasion for the church to relate to a stark reality. Although he said he could only ever be an Anglican, the illness had taken him in and out of the Church of England. He had concluded that the church wasn't God, and that its only purpose was to facilitate a person's relationship with God. He had therefore felt obliged to define what or who God was.

"That involved me on my own personal search for which AIDS has been the catalyst," he explained. "There is an odd sort of peace. AIDS raises the spiritual questions like: Why was I born? Why am I dying? Why do I have this disease? Where is it going? Why is it happening to me? Is this some form of punishment? It may also raise other questions like, Who is God? What is God? or Is there an afterlife? No one gets out of this world without asking those questions at some point. I have decided that all the answers will have to stay with God because I can't work them out."

Jonathan died a few months later. Although I met him only twice, he struck me as a person of extraordinary courage with a quiet faith, honed on the anvil of fear and uncertainty. Seven years later, as I was sitting in a coffee house in the palm-lined Castro district of San Francisco, he came into my mind again as I got up to greet Gregory Matracia, with whom I was to have my next conversation. As we shook hands and shared a joke, it was hard to believe that Gregory (wearing a bright orange baseball cap) had been HIV-positive for fourteen years and lived every day as if it were his last. Although he received the diagnosis at a time when people in San Francisco were frightened of being tested, the stark realization had nonetheless come as a shock. "The doctor breaks the news, you take it on board and then there comes a period when you begin to wonder how long your life is," he told me. "I worked at a gift store in the Castro but it's no longer here. The owners all passed away. Dead. AIDS took its toll here. I lost a lot of friends. Sometimes I get into a very dark place and wonder why I am still here when the friends I loved and my lover have all passed away."

Gregory, who was in his late thirties when he was diagnosed, said his whole outlook on life and his view of the world had been turned inside out. Things he had considered important abruptly lost their significance. He found himself re-evaluating his priorities, such as the status of having a job, being professional, and indulging in the materialistic pleasures of life. Like Jonathan, what took on greater relevance were the existential questions of the self: Who he was and why he was here; indeed, why was anyone here at all? It was an inner reflection on why he did the things he did and what there was left to accomplish. He had always believed that, in order to change the world, he had first to change himself.

"I decided to get tested after caring for the first person I knew to be sick with the virus," said Gregory. "He called me on my birthday in 1988. He was in the hospital and had nowhere to go. He was one of my best friends from Kentucky where I grew up. He was homeless and had not told anybody he was ill. I started visiting him and he got a little better. Then I took him into my home. But all sorts of other problems arose because my housemates, who were themselves gay, didn't like him living there. The prejudice against gay HIV-positive people was rampant, even among the gay community itself."

The anxious friends moved out but Gregory stayed and nursed his pal until the day he died. That was the first time he had dealt with death on a personal level. At the same time his father, back in Kentucky, was also dying. But it was impossible for Gregory to visit him as well because his time and energies were expended looking after his friend, who urged Gregory to have an HIV test. It was only after his friend's death in 1989 that Gregory received his own diagnosis. He began the AZT treatment immediately but did not respond well, so he refused all medications. In the end, worsening health forced him to stop work in 1993. He was growing weaker by the day and knew that, if he were to survive, he would have to consent to drug therapy.

These days he has to take only two AIDS medications. He has developed a resistance to the rest, even though he has tried them all. He says he is "just sailing along," waiting for new drugs to become available. His body does not absorb fat so, when he doesn't eat, he rapidly loses weight. He has to remind himself to have meals because he is never hungry. "My mornings are spent in the bathroom. I can't leave the house until after eleven o'clock because I have to stay there. I have to take medication so I don't have accidents if I go out on the street."

But the diagnosis also had a more positive effect on him in that it triggered a new spiritual exploration. Gregory had a Catholic upbringing but stopped attending Mass during his high school days. Everything preached had been fear-fuelled and focused on ways of avoiding hell. So he had moved away from Roman Catholicism. But, after attending a reception in the hall of the all-inclusive Most Holy Redeemer (a church in the Castro), following a lesbian commitment ceremony in a San Francisco park, he felt particularly secure in being able to receive the sacrament of Holy Communion alongside other gay people. He said he now had a ministry of his own as a volunteer in the AIDS office, on the board of the AIDS support group and helping out in the church garden.

"I just started to live in the moment," he reflected philosophically. "I went into therapy so I could discover who I was as a person and what motivated me. My therapist helped me live for the day and not worry about what was going to happen tomorrow. So I try to stay in the moment and experience everything in that moment. That's the way everybody should live. My HIV diagnosis has made me self-evaluate and has given me a different view of what's important. It's not what you have, who your friends are, what career you have or what kind of car you drive. It's what kind of person you are. I don't believe my personality as such has changed but I have grown as a person.

"When I was going through therapy, I realized God was not some mystical being in heaven but was internal to me. When the church makes pronouncements that make me angry, I realize I am not the institutional church but a child of God. As far as Vatican statements on homosexuality are concerned, the Curia has to realize God makes people differently. God created us. He does not make mistakes. God is our father and any good parent loves their children no matter what they do. I think church teaching has caused great emotional damage to gay people. I think we would have many more people getting involved in the church if it stepped back and realized what was going on in the world. Jesus was bucking the system all the time. He was an anarchist. That's what they lose sight of. As human beings we are supposed to change and the church should change. Something has gone wrong."

Gregory has cared for many friends in their last months and been with them as they breathed their last. He is not confident about his long-term prospects. "I prepared for my own death when I was diagnosed," he told me. "I got my life in order. I have everything set up for my death. I am going to be cremated. It's all paid for. My will is made and locked up. I don't want a Requiem Mass. I'll be dead. I'll be in a better place. Funerals and memorials are not for the dead. They're for the living.

"When my lover, Paul, was dying, he wanted to know what I thought heaven was like. He was raised as a Catholic but no longer went to church. I know he believed in God but he had a fear of the afterlife. I told him that heaven was basically what you wanted it to be. It was what you felt would give you eternal bliss and joy. As humans we have no idea but, to placate ourselves, in our minds we make heaven what we want it to be. I have no idea what life after death is going to be like. I don't try to think about it because I have no idea. Nobody knows whether their ideas about it are right or wrong."

So fifty-year-old Gregory is content to live a life of perpetual gratitude, giving thanks at the beginning and close of each new day. "My prayer to God is to try to be the best person I can be for today," he explains. "God gave us this life to live it to the best of our ability. Through my illness, God has come alive again for me and has brought me back to the church. I have found him or maybe he's found me. I think God always comes and finds you."

thirteen

A Song of Liberation

"My past hasn't been smooth," admitted the Dean of Cape Town, "but through it all there has been God's sufficient grace." The Very Reverend Rowan Smith declared his homosexuality publicly in 1994, the year of the first democratic general election in South Africa. It happened at a family gathering during a discussion on the new constitution, which prohibits any form of discrimination including sexuality.

At the time, Rowan was serving on Archbishop Desmond Tutu's staff. "He was wonderfully affirming when I told him I was gay," said Rowan. "It was the Archbishop who had said that the apartheid regime should have banned the Bible, for here was our affirmation that we were all made in the image of God and were God's children through baptism. This is important to remember in the light of the current debate in the Anglican Church and the move to exclude gay and lesbian people by reason of their sexual orientation. In my own case, there has been oppression from fellow clergy and parishioners but always the desire to respect and honor one another."

Born in 1943, Rowan spent his early years in Cape Town, where he grew up with the apartheid label "Cape Colored," which was specified by the nationalist government. It indicated that he was of mixed descent. During his high school days, Rowan became more politically minded through the influence of his teachers who were opposed to "Colored Education." Most appeared pleased when, on matriculation, Rowan indicated that he felt called to the ordained ministry. When he moved to London to start training, he became aware that the limitations placed on him in South Africa were unrelated to his ability to accomplish, but merely concerned the color of his skin and political labeling. The apartheid regime had already helped to make him politically aware, and, while in England, he was encouraged by the civil rights movement in the United States. After ordination back in South Africa in his mid-twenties, Rowan served as a priest in the Cape Town diocese for ten years. The parishioners were "Cape Colored" like him. His second curacy was in a newly created parish for residents who had been moved from "Whites Only" areas.

But in 1977 Rowan opted for a change of direction, joining the Community of the Resurrection at Mirfield, West Yorkshire, whose monks had been active in South Africa since 1912. One of its most celebrated, Father Trevor Huddleston, became president of the Anti-Apartheid Movement. "I went to Mirfield believing there was much to be gained by working with a religious community," he told me. "But before leaving South Africa, I came out to my friends and hosted gay parties. There were those who saw my going to Mirfield as a cop-out. They thought I was running away from my sexuality."

Rowan went on, "It was in the novitiate that we were in fact encouraged to engage with our sexuality before we took vows of celibacy. It was then that I prayed to God to take away my homosexuality, not realizing that the vow applied equally to heterosexual and homosexual brethren. I shared this struggle with the novice guardian, who asked what would happen if God answered me in the same way as he had St Paul—'My grace is sufficient for you.' This grace was experienced in my accepting that, as with my color, this too was a given identity that brought its own freedom. God is so gracious. Who would have thought that having to deal with the vow of celibacy would be the means of embracing my homosexuality? I found it brought healing but the struggle is still ongoing. There is, from within me, a desire to give expression to my spirituality based on my own sexual experience and growth in self-acceptance of who I am as a man."

Such wrestling could assist others who, for whatever reason, had to live alone, suggested Rowan. It could help in trying to make sense of a God who loved people in their celibacy and could clarify how they should love their neighbor when they were not in an intimate relationship with another person. The church could learn from any expression of people's experience which evolved from their relationships and from their sexuality, especially in terms of how they responded to the Gospel.

The roots of homosexuality lay as much in Africa as anywhere else, Rowan pointed out. In some African societies, there had been an acceptance of older men training younger men through initiation rites to become fully male. Part of the process meant having a sexual relationship with them. Even though the term *homosexuality* was never used, there was an implicit understanding and acceptance of that kind of relationship. If people turned to the Acts of the Apostles, he said, they would see that one of the earliest converts to the Christian faith was a person who was described as an Ethiopian eunuch. Although the precise nature of his physical operation was unknown, here was an African who would not normally have been acceptable to those within the Jewish faith.

"I sincerely hope Africa has something to teach the Anglican Communion about diversity," Rowan said. "I hope there can also be an openness on the part of those who say homosexuality is un-African to ask themselves whether they are really responding as Africans—or as those who have received the Christian faith from a particular point of view. For example, are they objecting to homosexuality because the missionaries' interpretation of Scripture said that what some Africans were practicing was wrong? It was the missionaries who described as pagan and anti-Christian practices long accepted within the culture. Perhaps we need to go back and ask: were these practices in existence before the missionaries came and are we simply saying that our response today has been colored by that missionary experience?

"The missionaries, who came from Britain, brought with them their cultural baggage and failed to distinguish between the values of the Gospel and 'British' behavior. As Africans, we are being called by God to share our understanding of *Ubuntu* with the world and *ubuntu*, in part, translates as 'you are a person through other persons,' irrespective of gender, color or sexual orientation. We have experienced liberation from slavery and colonialism. As Saint Paul wrote to the Galatians, we should not now enslave ourselves by culture or tradition, especially if we then deny our God-given humanity."

Rowan said the political history of South Africa had been based on a lie that "color decided our worth." Now some members of the Anglican Church were saying that gay people were not only disqualified from leadership but, in Africa, did not exist at all. The head of the Anglican Church in South Africa, Archbishop Njongonkulu Ndungane, had stated that adopting a hard-line stance on the issue did nothing to enhance church unity. Listening to both sides was necessary because there was hurt on both sides. But the Archbishop had been criticized because he had dared to challenge the monolithic view of African sexuality which, even among Christians, included polygamy. To resort to talking about excommunication or of condemning one another to hell for "being satanic" did not give God the glory, nor did it enable people to welcome Christ in the other. "The church is always at pains to avoid fragmentation but there comes a point when its members have to face questions of justice, consider what the gospel response should be to a particular situation and ask whether that should be sacrificed for the sake of unity," he commented.

Gay and lesbian people had a significant contribution to make in encouraging and enabling all people to love and accept themselves for who they were. There had been times—still in existence in some parts of Africa—when culture had been used to diminish the status of women and abuse them. "If we can own who we are, we can actually set free some of the more culturally bound males who think that the only way in which one can be a person is to be a dominant male and exclude everybody else—women and children as well as gay and lesbian people," he said. "We have a very important contribution to make in the liberation of our continent by telling others to love and accept themselves as they are and enjoy who they are as sexual beings. The Gospel is about setting people free. It is about claiming that 'the Spirit of God is upon me because he has anointed me.' That Spirit belongs to everyone by virtue of their baptism and we are to celebrate the liberation that Jesus Christ has brought us."

As Dean of Cape Town, Rowan Smith believes he has been the

recipient of "a goodly heritage" because both his predecessors and his church have stood in opposition to injustice and discrimination. Life is a gift. And for Rowan that includes the color of his skin as well as the nature of his sexuality. That he has come so far is "all grace." No matter how he might stumble along the pilgrim way, there is always the joy of that grace which is God's free gift to each person through Christ Jesus.

Rowan says he has had to be true to his vocation as someone created in God's image—and faithful to what he believes the Gospel is calling the church to proclaim: that fullness of life in Christ Jesus is for every person, regardless of their ethnicity, class or sexual orientation.

"We are all wounded people and, like our Savior, Jesus Christ, we bear the scars of our past," he told me. "I have been able to celebrate God's grace in my brokenness as a person of color and likewise I see homosexuality as a gift. This is in line with the Christian understanding that all life is gift and that, according to Genesis 1, 'God saw all that God had made, and behold it was very good.'

"God has indeed blessed me through that which others have rejected."

fourteen

Maternal Instincts

"When I read statements from the Vatican about gay unions being evil," declared Roz Gallo, "I wonder how many of those men have seen a relationship that is working. We have respect, integrity and all the components of a real marriage."

We were conversing in a comfortable apartment in the Mission district of San Francisco, where fifty-one-year-old Roz lives with her partner, Catherine Cunningham, sixty. Both are Catholic mothers who struggled to bring up their children alone after the failure of their marriages. They had to overcome many psychological, spiritual, and financial hurdles along the way but, through their trials and sacrifices, feel they have come to understand more clearly what loving is all about.

"I am a much happier and more stable person than I was in my earlier years," said Roz, a native of Los Angeles, who married at the age of twenty but soon began to suspect she had made "a dreadful mistake." By then she was pregnant, but she remained in the marriage for fifteen years, exploring her sexuality with women at the same time. "The marriage wasn't sacramental. It wasn't union. At best we might have been friends but it was pretty awful. Had there been more openness about homosexuality in my younger days, I might not have wed. I had a sense of the alternatives but, as a good Catholic girl, I would never have thought of exploring them."

Brought up in a suburb of Chicago, Catherine married at twenty-nine and had two sons. She divorced at the age of thirty-six and began living as a single parent, but has remained close to her former husband, Al, and his family. "Coming out for me was much easier than it was for Roz," she explained. "I always thought that living as a bisexual would be the way forward for me because it was less limiting. I didn't struggle with being gay as she did. I was a single mother raising two kids. I didn't have a lot of money. That was the dark time for me, not dealing with my sexuality."

Roz and Catherine originally met in 1978 while they were still in their marriages. They noticed there was an instant rapport and the fact that each had a five-year-old child at the time bonded them at the maternal level. But it was another nine years before they formed a relationship. Through her involvement with the ecumenical Cursillo movement (which offers long-weekend courses to help people share and deepen their spiritual journeys), Roz began to explore her emerging homosexuality in relation to her faith. As a committed Catholic, it was crucial that, whatever changes were about to take place, her relationship with God should remain intact. Faith would be integral to the choices before her.

"While I didn't find any encouragement in the wider Catholic Church, there was a margin of support in Cursillo," she explained. "I kept feeling that my spiritual journey was putting me more in touch with my sexuality. I was moving closer to God and starting to have a greater understanding of my lesbian identity. But at the same time I had tremendous guilt because I believed very strongly in the sacrament of marriage. I had committed myself to it, even if I had been naive or uninformed at the time."

Roz even received the laying-on of hands from friends in the hope she would be healed of the guilt that was haunting her. While being a lesbian was not an infirmity as such, it seemed to her "almost like having leprosy," a disease that didn't exactly "mesh" with how she had been raised. "What emerged from a very deep level of prayer was the realization that healing was not, in fact, an appropriate response," she said. "God didn't desire that my true sexuality be exorcised from me. This was who God had created me to be. From that point on, I felt considerably freer in accepting who I was. I later went into therapy to try to understand myself more. The more I became clear about who I was, the healthier I became in terms of identifying myself as a lesbian person."

After a long struggle in her marriage, Roz separated from her husband in 1986. That same year, at the start of a Cursillo weekend, she spotted a familiar name on the list of candidates. After checking it was the same Catherine Cunningham she had met some years before, Roz sent a note to say she would be praying for her during the weekend. Before long they were connecting again and vowing to see each other more often. Roz learned that Catherine's younger son, Nathan, was in a hospital close to where she lived. As Catherine was driving down each weekend to visit him, the women decided they could develop their friendship by meeting for lunch or going to a concert. Sadly Nathan, who was eleven, died in December of that year.

Happier times lay ahead. Roz and Catherine were delighted to discover they were working on the same Cursillo team the following May. They spent a good deal of time preparing work together and grew much closer, but Catherine remained hesitant about deepening the relationship. On the Saturday morning of that Cursillo weekend, she was "awakened by a bolt of lightning" and received a clear message that said, "Don't be a fool. Don't walk away from this."

But as Roz and Catherine finally became partners, they realized the next hurdle would be telling the children. They sensed it might not run smoothly. Roz's daughter, Rena, and Catherine's son, Jeremiah, were both turning fourteen. "Rena was really upset," Roz told me. "I'd gone to visit for the weekend. We'd been to the ocean and had a summer picnic. As we were leaving, my ex-husband turned to me and said, 'By the way, I found this note Rena wrote to a school friend. It says, *Oh my God. I think my mother's a lesbian.*'"

Roz insisted she and Rena should talk things through there and then. She took her daughter for a car ride and attempted an explanation she felt was long overdue. But so stunned was Rena by the confirmation of her suspicions that the only words she could utter were, "I don't want to hear this now." Roz tried to elaborate but Rena declined to discuss it further. It was another nine months before the conversation could resume. By chance Rena discovered a school pal in the same boat. Her friend's mother was also a lesbian, and the sharing that went on between them helped Rena immensely in her coming to terms with the reality.

For Jeremiah, the shock was cushioned by the fact that he had been educated at an alternative school where several of the teachers had been gay or lesbian. Moreover, they were some of his mother's closest friends. "I finally told Jeremiah that I had fallen in love with Roz when he was a freshman in high school," explained Catherine. "We were in the car coming across the Golden Gate Bridge in San Francisco. I got the silent treatment to begin with so all I had to do was to drive him to his father's house in the city. Al was already in the picture. When I walked in with Jeremiah, I said to Al despondently, 'Well, I told Jeremiah the news and he's just *thrilled* about it.' Al replied, 'Well, I have been thinking about this and I really *am* thrilled. I just think this is wonderful. I am so glad you have found somebody you can love and who makes you happy.' So Jeremiah didn't have a lot of room to be snotty about it! He had to get on with it—which he did within a week. Soon we became the token lesbians and he had to show us off to his friends."

Although their faith journeys had taken different courses for different reasons over the years, the new couple began to search in earnest for an appropriate parish. Already familiar with the Taizé "Prayer Around the Cross" from the ecumenical Taizé religious community based in France, they learned that Most Holy Redeemer in the Castro district of San Francisco was incorporating this solemnity into an annual "Forty Hours' Devotion" focusing on a cure for AIDS. It sounded promising. They turned up eagerly and found the service "moving and beautiful." It was a life-changing experience that enabled them to claim their Catholicism and their sexuality in full equal measure for the first time.

They discovered that lesbian and gay people comprised three-quarters of the congregation and some brought along their adopted children. At last, this was a community of faith where they could feel loved, accepted and fully involved, a place they could call home. They have since served on a variety of committees and helped the church-rebuilding project. Roz, who was formerly president of the parish council, is now a reader, while Catherine is an acolyte. For Roz, every Sunday Mass is "an experience of God real and present," something not previously experienced by her in the Catholic Church.

"I work in a corporation. I think I understand institutions—and the church as an institution has some learning to do," she pointed out. "It is a model of its time, yet it can never be forward thinking until it starts listening to the people. If I see the church institution as the business part, I can separate myself from it. That doesn't define me. It's the people of God who help define who I am and what my relationships are. I pray for those men at the Vatican, including the Pope, that they might see more broadly. I won't find fault with them because I can't judge their approach. But I pray that their minds be opened. As a woman in the church and as a lesbian in the church, there is plenty to be unhappy about. But, if I harbor that anger, it prevents me from feeling I have a place at the table."

Roz is convinced she and Catherine have become "better human beings" because of their open and committed lesbian relationship. "We try to be responsible citizens, good mothers and kind to folks who can use our help," she said. "When we worked with people living with HIV/AIDS, I think we gave those men a sense of comfort because we are maternal people. Our mothering was able to come through to them. Often their own mothers had rejected them and we could be a substitute for some of that."

Both believe they are better parents themselves because they are so much happier together than they were as single mothers struggling alone with young children. There is a fullness in their lives that allows them to see beyond the boxes in which they were raised. They sense their children, now thirty, would not be the creative filmmakers they are today if they too had been subjected to a confined childhood. The couple had provided them with insights that were different. Rena now lives in Los Angeles and Jeremiah in New York. Even though they are far apart, they relate like brother and sister and enjoy a very close relationship. "We treat them as people," said Catherine. "We try to be open, understanding and thoughtful, honoring them as adults."

"The suffering I have experienced has forced me to be more

open-minded and to prioritize. It has meant sacrifice, understanding and looking beyond the black and white. And through the love I have for Roz, I have learned more than I have ever done about how God loves me. The people I am surrounded by in church are to me the tangible presence of God."

Roz, too, feels she is able to communicate with God with less anxiety, an ever-present relationship from which she draws strength. "We have come through a lot and we are able to meet adversity in a way that is different," she added. "We have much to be grateful for. We are ordinary folk who have been blessed. Together I think we can handle anything. That comes from being tested by fire."

fifteen

Greek Fire

"Faith does everything," Milos exclaimed. "Just look up there. Nobody knows how they live or survive."

The young Orthodox guide was taking me on a tour of Mount Athos, the autonomous monastic republic in Greece where only men may tread. We were on a steep road dedicated to the prophet Elijah, admiring majestic views of the turquoise Aegean. The twenty-six-year-old pilgrim told me how Athos had regained its position as the spiritual powerhouse of the Orthodox world, unyielding in its adherence to tradition. Some of the two thousand monks, he pointed out, lived in isolated sketes or villages dotted across the hilly terrain. A world of its own, the atmosphere was tranquil and unthreatening. At every turn, sweet-smelling incense mingled with the scent of spring flowers and the sound of birdsong. The noise of a drill seemed somewhat incongruous until I learned that the Holy Mountain even had its own dental clinic adorned with icons of the Virgin Mary, smiling down on terrified patients.

It was Easter and the guest house had provided little chocolate eggs for us at breakfast. "Christ is risen," proclaimed Milos as he tapped his egg against mine. "Christ is risen, indeed," I replied. I was struck by his joyful spirituality, his love of God and his devotion to the Virgin. He prayed with me, instructed me in the eastern spiritual tradition and tried gently to convert me to Orthodox Christianity. We spoke about our beliefs long into the night, keeping as quiet as church mice for fear of waking the brothers who had gone to bed much earlier.

On the day of my departure, we continued our mystical conversation along a mountain pathway, marveling again at the magnificent vistas in every direction. Passing through a gateway, Milos suddenly stopped. He looked downcast. Anxiety had eclipsed his spirit. Tentatively, he asked if he could share something. Sighing, he told me how he adored the Orthodox Church but could never feel fully part of it. He felt drawn and alienated at the same time. Then he revealed that he was gay, had been in a relationship, and was struggling to reconcile a passionate sexuality with an equally intense spirituality. "You see, my church takes a very hard line on practicing homosexuals," he explained. "I love this holy mountain but the monks here would not approve of my lifestyle. They adhere strictly to tradition."

But Milos did not divulge what I later discovered from an Orthodox priest in Britain: that two monks from Athos had died of AIDS in the 1980s, a scandal that had swept through the mainland press like Greek fire. "I can understand the dilemma Milos was in," said seventy-three-year-old Father Spyridon, a celibate homosexual who works in a British university. "All the Orthodox churches regard homosexual practice as objectively wrong."

The priest handed me a tract, *The Homosexual Christian*, published by the Department of Religious Education for the Orthodox Church in America. In bold language, it stated that the Orthodox Church identified solidly with those Christians who regard homosexual orientation as "a disorder and disease, and who therefore consider homosexual actions as sinful and destructive." Homosexual Christians were called to a "particularly rigorous battle." Their struggle was "an especially ferocious one," not made any easier by the "mindless, truly demonic hatred of those who despise and ridicule those who carry this painful and burdensome cross; nor by the mindless, equally demonic affirmation of homosexual activity by its misguided advocates and enablers."

The leaflet stressed that, like all temptations, passions, and sins, including those "deeply and oftentimes seemingly indelibly embedded in our nature by our sorrowful inheritance," a homosexual orientation could be cured and homosexual actions could cease. When homosexual Christians were willing to struggle, with compassionate and loving assistance from families and friends, the Lord guaranteed victory "in ways known to Himself."

No wonder the Greek Orthodox pilgrim on Mount Athos looked so tortured, for I sensed he was drawn either to priesthood or the monastic life itself. He knew he could never be healed of his sexuality. It had led him into a beautiful relationship of trust and commitment. He felt torn between love and guilt.

Father Spyridon said that when he counseled young people about their homosexual feelings, he told them it was a matter of having to live with their drives and emotions. God had made them gay. If they were left-handed, they were left-handed. If they had a squint, they had a squint. They had to accept the fact. But what they did about it was ultimately up to them. "They will probably fall, especially if they do not have a promise to live up to," he said. "People who live with homosexuality have a problem. If they are going to live perfectly as Orthodox Christians, they are going to have to keep away from sex."

The priest did not think that homosexuality could be intrinsically disordered or evil, as the Roman Catholic Church maintained, because God did not make people evil and nobody chose to be gay. "But I don't look on homosexuality as a gift," he added. "It's a fact. And if you talk about the wound of homosexuality, it suggests you are injured or have a disease.

"I feel the vulnerability of students who are gay and those who think I might be gay," he confessed. "They could put me in a very difficult position. I wouldn't be open about being gay because most people would find it offensive. I would lose a lot of altar credibility. I don't ask other people if they are gay so why should they want to know about me? Some wonder, some suspect and some definitely know."

Father Spyridon was sixteen when he suspected he was homosexual but he sublimated his feelings. When he went off to train in his forties he still kept silent. Nobody asked him directly about his sexuality. It was never an issue. The Orthodox Church certainly embraced homosexuals among its clergy and laity, but the prevailing attitude was one of "Don't ask. Don't tell."

When he was ordained at the age of forty-four, he had to promise that he would abstain from all sexual activity. "I am bound by that," he said. "But it gets very depressing when I find out that other people, gay and straight, are enjoying a sexual life and I cannot. The consolation comes when I realize nobody would ever want an old carthorse like me!"

sixteen

Intimacy and Distance

As a gay canon in the Church of England, Simon felt a natural empathy for Jeffrey John, of Southwark Cathedral, when evangelical pressure forced the respected theologian to withdraw from his appointment as Bishop of Reading. "I sent him a letter, offering support and prayers," said Simon. "It was all very sad and not the way the church should be operating in the public domain. The initial announcement was a great encouragement to those of us who saw this as a progressive move. But it became clear that the local churches in the Diocese of Oxford weren't ready for it. However, although the ultimate decision was not ideal, I think that, for the time being, it was the right one."

Simon has not been in a long-term relationship for many years. Nonetheless he told me that this had "nothing to do with being a morally upright priest who obeys the church's teaching on homosexuality." It was simply because he valued his own space and liked living on his own. Moreover, he would not want to be categorized as "celibate" and would not flinch from entering a relationship in the future. Neither would he flaunt it. He would want to be sensitive to his partner, his bishop, and the church while being careful to protect his own boundaries. "Gay relationships should not be lived secretly," he insisted.

Cathedral life is a world away from Simon's own family upbringing among the rough diamonds of a mining community. There was always an assumption in his home village that boys would follow their fathers down the pits. But Simon's mother was adamant her elder son would not be one of them. She believed he was probably too sensitive a person to work alongside the miners. After all, she always recalled the day she had observed him playing in a garden.

"I got dirt on my hands," said Simon. "I ran inside crying and asked my mother to wash it off. I think she knew I would never make a miner if I couldn't even cope with a little dirt on my hands. The story was often retold by my mother to indicate her knowledge that I was gay. Perhaps it was her way of saying that she knew and it was okay by her. She communicated it with a smile on her face. It was, perhaps, the only way she had of expressing her gift of total acceptance back to me."

Simon grew up with an intense dislike of rugby and football but with a gift for music and writing stories, even though his tales of horror would often alarm his sister. But he was unable to frighten off the local boys who, like his father, taunted him with insults directed against a creativity they considered unmanly. "My father tried to teach me cricket once, but I only lasted a few minutes. I left the team bored and went home to play the piano. When my father got back he told me I would never be a real man showing off on that thing. Why hadn't I stayed and played the man's games? My mother really tore into him about that. While my mother, grandmothers and aunts encouraged me with my music, my father and schoolmates continued to be abusive. This led to a shy, unhappy childhood."

The eldest of three, Simon became particularly close to his mother. They always baked cakes together and, because money was short, experimented with making gifts at Christmas for friends and relatives. "My mother and I always talked about everything and anything," said Simon. "Nothing was hidden." Their closeness was "one of the most non-sexual intimate relationships I have had," but it was a bonding that came to be resented by Simon's father.

"I recall great jealousy from my father toward my mother and me," Simon recalled. "When I was beginning my adolescence, at the age of about fourteen, there was a horrendous argument one night after I had gone to bed. When I asked my mother what it was all about, she told me that he had accused her and I of a sexual relationship." So, as Simon moved from childhood into adulthood, he began to distance himself from the intimacy he had experienced.

"She always cut our hair, but one day she began playing with mine rather than cutting it. I felt most uncomfortable about this 'sexual' act, although I did not understand it at the time. I told her to stop. She became very angry with me and accused me of not loving her any more. With hindsight, it had become an inappropriate intimacy. I think she had transferred some of the husband/career role onto me as her first-born. I was always her favorite."

During his teenage years his mother suffered from severe depression, so at fifteen Simon left school to nurse her. He also had to cook, clean, and shop, ensuring there was always food on the table when other members of the family got home. This allowed his mother to sleep and be "comatose in her depression." Simon became the matriarch of the family, but the psychological pressures of coming to terms with his nascent homosexuality led to a breakdown when he was nineteen. When he explicitly told his mother some years later that he was gay, she was not surprised, although she was forced to confront a reality she had only ever surmised.

Simon's father had been "a very absent presence." At the age of twenty, Simon joined the army in search, he suspects, of a male figure long missing in his life. But he was unhappy in Germany. He battled his way through two years of personal isolation before deciding to move back to England to study. "It was during my time at college that I experienced more interior struggles with my sexuality and wrestled with my own depressions," he told me. "These came to the surface through my life of prayer. I was practicing silence and the art of simply being who I was before God."

Unable to make sense of what he was experiencing, the twenty-four-year-old found a spiritual director and began to experience the sacraments as "great gifts of grace." Through careful guidance and the liturgy of the church, Simon gradually discovered his true self. Then he stumbled across Henri Nouwen's *Reaching Out*, which was to bring him much solace and encouragement.[1] It became a reference book to which he returned again and again. Its message brought meaning into his confused life. In the book, Nouwen understands the spiritual life as a constantly flowing movement between polarities: between the poles of loneliness and solitude (the relationship to oneself); hostility and hospitality (the relationship to others); and between illusion and prayer (the relationship with God). In a simple yet profound way, the writer spoke to Simon's heart in its bewilderment.

Like Nouwen, Simon experienced his life as a constant state of movement and change. He desired intimacy yet feared it. He wanted aloneness, but craved companionship. "I was struggling with depression, the church's view of homosexuality and a strong desire to be still and alone with God," he said. "Nouwen's writing resonated, with profound reality and integrity. Here was a man who articulated my personal struggles with clarity, gentleness and empathy." The polarities also connected with Simon's subsequent experience of being both a priest and a gay man. "These polarities of self had sometimes torn away so negatively that I wondered who I was," he said. "But Nouwen reminded me that I could not bypass these. I was faced with three polarities of my own: being internally depressed while presenting myself as the whole and competent minister and student; between having to be the expected heterosexual and therefore being the suppressed homosexual if I wanted to fulfill what I considered to be a vocation to the priesthood; and between being a rather shy and private man, yet also a public and, therefore, expected-to-be hospitable figure, now a possession of others."

For fifteen years Simon lived in a gay relationship with Chris. Simon's mother included him as an equal member of the family. No questions were asked and there was an atmosphere of unconditional acceptance. When she died suddenly, Simon was understandably devastated. The last words he spoke to her, a few days before her death, were "I love you." She responded, "I love you too." It proved a moving valediction because nobody else in the family had ever told Simon's mother that they loved her. He wondered if his innate sensitivity and understanding as a gay person had brought them closer, as friends as well as son and mother. It was not until his wife's death that the father could cease fighting or competing for Simon's attention. "With mother absent, father could become closer," he explained. "As time has gone on, a strange reversal has occurred. There has been a welcome reconciliation between my father and me. This was what my mother always wanted. It is a shame she never saw it."

But Simon was to suffer more grief with the break-up of his relationship. The pain of separation from Chris was acute. "The cost of losing a loved one, effectively through a divorce, was very hard indeed, as anyone who breaks a relationship will know," he lamented. "It is no different for those of us who are gay. We need time to heal." Even though the break-up with Chris had been "heart-wrenching," he still believed love was "worth the risks."

Reflecting on recent developments in the Anglican Communion, Simon pointed out that it had been his mother who had taught him that feelings were paramount. People had to take care of their own emotions as well as those of others. If "Mother Church" could emulate this attitude, her gift to gay people would be precious indeed. Gay and lesbian Christians were currently experiencing the birth pangs of "Mother Church" attempting to welcome into her community homosexuals who "faithfully and willingly give their gift of love to her and the world." He said people in cathedrals and parish churches longed to see this slow birth moving "to a place of cradling embrace." Gay people were, in some ways, similar to members of the Christian feminist movement who had challenged the institution's patriarchal nature to "bring the wall of prejudice and power tumbling down," and breathe new life into a dying body. "We are called by God to serve, whether by being politically active in changing unjust laws or by offering compassion for those who suffer injustice themselves," said Simon. "We know first hand the struggles for liberation and coming out without fear of abuse. But we should never return abuse to those who are prejudiced. We bring to the church a powerful story of compassion, love and struggle. What I can bring as a gay priest is an honesty about the depth of my compassion—and passion—for others. I always make connections with the gospel story of Christ. What my witness offers, as a gay man who happens to be a priest called by the church, is the sense of ephrathta—'be opened.' This means opening out to a greater honesty about being a human being or giving permission for others to be themselves publicly, without risk of judgment. I have been honest. I have been opened. I have also been broken. I bring to other people a celebration of life in all its beauty as best I can."

seventeen

Unholy Orders

"I've been physically, mentally and sexually abused in my life," said Martin, a former Roman Catholic seminarian. "Now I feel I have been spiritually abused as well."

The year 2004 was unfolding and, as he supped mild ale in an English country pub, Martin hoped he would not have to endure another difficult year. For a man of thirty-four, he had witnessed too many of those already. If everything had gone according to plan, Martin would have been nearing his ordination. He had always felt a calling to priesthood, and the Roman Catholic Church had recognized his many spiritual and pastoral qualities. Clasping his hands around the tankard, he sighed as he told me how he now delivered toilet rolls for a living.

At a time when the church's attitude toward gay seminarians was becoming a talking point, especially among young people considering vocations, Martin said he felt he had been discriminated against because he was a homosexual, even though he had never flaunted his orientation. He claimed gay people were being actively discouraged from joining the ranks of the clergy because homosexuality was being erroneously associated with pedophilia in some parts of the church. Martin said he had met many people who had either been turned down for ministry or been asked to leave their seminaries because they were openly gay. Ironically, at the other end of the spectrum, he knew of gay priests who refused to conceal their homosexuality in church circles and did not always live up to their vows of celibacy.

Martin explained how, as a youngster, he had been fully

involved in the activities of his parish. After leaving school, he had taken a variety of jobs but thoughts of full-time committed service to the church had been unremitting. After a four-year process of discernment, the sense of vocation had been as strong as ever and he had decided to offer himself for training. Accepted by the church authorities, he had been sent to a seminary in Britain.

"I worked hard, got on with everybody, excelled at the pastoral placements and it all seemed to be going well," said Martin. "I realized that seminary life was part of my formation and I absorbed every minute of it. It had its difficult spells but all the painstaking effort was worth it because it felt right."

During those first two years of formation, when students were encouraged to reflect on matters of personal integration, Martin realized he had a long-standing anxiety over his sexuality, so he raised the issue with his spiritual director, one of the college lecturers. He recommended that Martin seek counseling to become more at ease with who he was as a sexual being. During a year of confidential, weekly meetings, a woman counselor unearthed "a host of concerns" about Martin's sexual development. She was convinced he had been abused before the age of four. It was a shocking disclosure. The seminarian was distraught. "I had to think of every close family member and friends who had been involved in my childhood, reliving all those fond memories with a painful agenda," he said. "This included the happy times I had spent with my late father who had loved me very much. I had to ask myself whether he or any of them could have done such damage to me. It was terrible."

Martin admitted to the counselor that, during his childhood and early adolescence, he had had experiences with adults of both sexes. Some of these encounters had been with priests and married men. Through the sessions he learned that many of these people had probably been taking advantage of him for their own needs without his realizing. That too was a frightening revelation. The counselor helped him to see that what he had always understood as friendships had in fact been forms of abuse. Although the picture was not in full focus, Martin inwardly rejoiced that, for the first time, he was being put in touch with realities that lay hidden deep in the psyche. It was like the "partial unveiling of a gift."

Throughout this period Martin kept the college principal updated on his progress. At the time, he felt he owed him that allegiance because the seminary was supporting him as well as footing the bill. Martin was so grateful for these self-discoveries that he decided (perhaps unwisely, he now thinks) to share with the principal all he was learning about his past.

The counselor later suggested that Martin ought to be assessed by a more experienced therapist. The college principal spent some weeks trying to locate the right person, eventually securing the name of a forensic psychologist. But when Martin and the principal turned up at a hospital clinic, they became somewhat disconcerted that some of his regular clients appeared to be pedophiles. Nonetheless, it was agreed that Martin should still undergo what turned out to be a series of "horrific psychological tests" geared more to child rapists than seminarians. At every session he was asked to answer scores of "sickening" questions that seemed entirely inappropriate. He found himself in a constant state of bewilderment because he had been eager for a more specialized form of counseling, not a procedure that had been devised for criminal assessment.

The psychologist's report was sent to the principal. Even though it was the middle of the summer holidays, he summoned Martin to his office, a three-hour car journey away. There he was relieved to learn that the psychologist had concluded he was no danger to children. He was simply a gay man with a "high sex drive" who, like many priests, might find celibate life difficult. But the principal looked serious because the psychologist had also indicated that Martin would need ongoing support. This could only be provided at a "phenomenal" financial cost to the church. The key question was whether or not Martin's bishop would agree to pay out the money for a ministry that might last forty years. Martin was certain such therapy was unnecessary and considered the principal's reaction melodramatic. Martin merely wanted to own his new-found sexual identity so he could move into his priestly ministry with greater self-understanding and integrity.

A meeting was arranged with the bishop, who shocked Martin by informing him that he needed time away from the seminary. "I told him that I didn't think I had a problem," said Martin. "I didn't want ongoing therapy. I just wanted to get back to college and carry on with my training. But the bishop said he felt obliged to give me what he kept terming 'freedom.' He insisted that I had to get all notion of priesthood and vocation out of my head. I pointed out to him that, if that were the case, I wouldn't be able to go to Mass, worship or pray because all three were so deeply embedded within my sense of calling. I started talking about a year out, but the bishop said that, even if I came back in five or seven years, he would not recommend me for seminary unless something miraculous happened—whatever that meant.

"I felt destroyed. I went back home to my mother who was losing her battle against cancer. Her will to survive was centered on my vocation to the priesthood. There was an emptiness and confusion within me. I didn't know what to do next. I still had this strong sense of calling but I also felt flattened and rejected. I couldn't understand how the bishop had come to his decision and I didn't agree with it. There was a huge frustration on my part."

Martin told me that he had been devastated by the news that he could not return to the seminary. It all seemed so sudden and definitive. The psychologist's report had not been alarming. Perhaps, in the current climate, the bishop was not prepared to take risks with anyone. After getting transferred to a college nearer his home, Martin knuckled down to his theology degree as best he could and took a part-time job to make ends meet. But he had unquestionably lost his sense of identity.

Then one night, like a scene from a movie, two detectives turned up at his house with a warrant for his arrest. A prisoner who had been close to Martin in his younger days and whom Martin had visited in jail had made allegations of indecent assault against him. He knew Martin had been training to be a priest and was possibly aware of the compensation money that the Roman Catholic Church was handing out to victims of abuse. Martin wondered if he might have been trying his luck. He was mortified by the accusations, which he knew to be false, and fearful that reputations could be so easily destroyed by unsubstantiated claims. In the end the police decided not to arrest him but said they would look into the matter further. This resulted in a seven-month investigation in which the college principal was interviewed and the bishop kept informed.

"I had never been through anything as frightening in my life," said Martin. "I became withdrawn because the detectives even wanted to question friends of mine who had children. One minute I had been training to be a priest, the next I was the subject of a criminal investigation. I felt angry and betrayed for a second time. I decided not to tell my mother because her health was deteriorating. I couldn't concentrate on anything. My part-time work suffered and my finals were approaching. I even contemplated suicide but thoughts of my mother's illness and the need to clear my name held me back. But every day I was tormented by the unknown. I knew I was innocent but I did not know what lay around the corner. It was indeed a dark night of the soul."

Despite the inner turmoil, Martin passed all his exams and began to look to the future. With encouragement from lecturers, priests and friends to carve out a career with young people, he applied for the post of a lay chaplain at a Catholic school and landed the job. He was the best candidate by far and the head teacher was delighted to have him on the staff. Life was suddenly more radiant. But on the very morning his mother died, the head called him to say that the governors would not consent to his appointment. They were confused because their instructions to turn him down had come "from sources above them." To Martin, these seemed like "unholy orders." The bishop had deemed him unsuitable for the post because, even though he had not been charged with any offense, there was an ongoing police investigation.

A few days later, Martin received a letter from the police, stating that no charges would be pressed. He immediately called the head teacher to try to retrieve the job but was told it was out of his hands. The head suspected there was another agenda afoot and advised Martin to uncover it because he feared his future job applications might be jeopardized. When Martin later confronted the bishop in person, he admitted Martin had been treated unfairly. But even though the investigation had closed and Martin's innocence had been accepted by the police, it was clear the bishop had no intention of reversing the decision.

"I could not believe my ears when he started saying I would be better off stacking shelves in Tesco's than thinking of jobs with pastoral responsibilities," said Martin. "I had been involved with the church all my life and had gained a theology degree. But I was getting the distinct impression that the bishop had an issue with my ever working with children. The psychological assessments hadn't indicated any problem in that regard. And by sheer coincidence, I had been falsely accused by an inmate whom I thought was a friend. I hadn't done anything wrong. I challenged the bishop but he evaded my questions. He said he was concerned about my vulnerability with groups of young people.

"I became convinced that the issue was really about my being gay. I broached this with the bishop and pointed out that my sexuality should not prevent me from working with children. After all, he had already prevented me from returning to seminary because a psychologist had concluded I was a gay man with a high sex drive. I am sure the church rejected me because I am homosexual, however much they wrapped it up in other language. I got the impression that the church was equating homosexuality with the potential for pedophilia which was not only outrageous but also insulting and destructive."

Martin told me that he had been prepared to lead a celibate life but would have been rejecting God had he denied his sexuality to himself. God had made him the person he was. "I just wanted to own a sexuality for myself because it had always been dictated to me by men who thought they already knew," he explained. "I could not have become a priest until and unless I was content with whatever that sexuality turned out to be. Other people, including the seminary principal, had always admired the fact that I was an honest and truthful person who had a variety of qualities that the church would benefit from. They even told me that such integrity would benefit me in difficult times. Now all that has gone against me.

"I consider all of this a form of spiritual abuse because it has interfered with my rightful development as a human being and with my personal relationship with God with whom I have always felt a deep bond. My conscience has obeyed the will of the One who calls. But I know there is a stumbling block that is beyond my control—the church's utter fear of homosexuality in an institution. During my time in seminary, we were all encouraged to come to terms with our sexuality as part of our journey to wholeness. I faced mine squarely and truthfully, then everything came crashing down because I was honest about exploring who I was as a person. It has been the worst period of my life. I carry this story around with me night and day. Sometimes I can't move because of its sheer weight. There are so few people I can discuss it with."

One of the most extraordinary ironies was that, in its treatment of him, the church had not appeared even to follow its own teaching, which clearly states that men and women with homosexual tendencies "must be accepted with respect, compassion and sensitivity. Every sign of unjust discrimination in their regard should be avoided."

Martin put his pint down on the table. "I have simply been dumped by the church," he said. "I feel abandoned. From being an aspiring priest for others, I have ended up selling toilet rolls. The institution hasn't shown any pastoral concern in helping me to heal or make sense of what has happened to me. It hasn't given me the slightest glimmer of hope. Yet, in spite of everything I have been through, my vocation to the priesthood is stronger than ever and I am prepared to go to the grave in pursuit of that calling."

eighteen

A Daring Confidence

Evangelical Christians Sigrid and Sylvia Rutishauser-James have been in a committed relationship for thirty years. They chose to unite their surnames and signed a partnership register for lesbian and gay couples. They define their relationship as "a coming together of two people in difference," a congruent friendship of which physical intimacy is a part.

"As a homosexual woman I have to stake my life on God because so many evangelicals say I am living wrongly," Sigrid told me at the couple's semi-detached home in the Cheshire town of Macclesfield, where the neighbors are more friendly and supportive than many in the church. "Most evangelicals are hesitant and uncertain how they should relate to us. Some speak with love, some with disagreement but most with reserve. So I have to place my faith in God, knowing that God understands what I don't understand. I have to live in that assurance."

While Sigrid said she had sometimes felt like abandoning the church, she could never cut herself off from her evangelical roots. For many years she and Sylvia have been actively involved with the Evangelical Fellowship for Lesbian and Gay Christians, which has more than a hundred members. The label *evangelical* was one Sigrid gladly wore both as a student and as a member of the Christian Union. These days she espouses it with even more conviction, drawing inspiration from a quotation of Martin Luther where the Reformer speaks about faith as "a living, daring confidence in God's grace, so sure and certain that the believer would stake his life on it a thousand times."

Sigrid acknowledges that, in the past, there has been great conflict between the relationship with Sylvia and her evangelical faith. But over the years her understanding of biblical criticism has matured and she despairs now when familiar verses are "trotted out" to condemn homosexual relationships. "I do not read these texts literally," she points out. "I regard them as contextually based and the best understanding people had in those days. I do not see them as immediately relevant to my life now. During the Jeffrey John episode, I felt exasperation, frustration and anger at the way the Bible was being used as an obstacle and a weapon to beat people over the head with. The Bible has in fact enriched my relationship by encouraging me not to fear or hide, and challenging me to be more open and to keep things in perspective."

Although Sigrid and Sylvia worship in Anglican churches, they have a Baptist background. Sigrid, a physiologist, grew up in Wembley, the daughter of Swiss and German parents. Sylvia, who was born in Cardiff, trained as a nurse and worked both in Uganda with the Medical Research Council and then in the Congo with the Baptist Missionary Society. While in Kampala she found herself working with Sigrid's sister. Sylvia first met her future partner when Sigrid visited Africa in 1965. Sylvia was then twenty-two and Sigrid, eighteen. Fixed in her memory is an image of Sigrid coming into the room where staff were gathering for morning coffee. "There was for me, in my first meeting with Sigrid, what I can only describe as a recognition," Sylvia recalled. The impact of the encounter could not be described rationally, she said. The word *homosexuality* was absent from most people's vocabulary in those days. She simply felt she *knew* Sigrid.

Going along to the Medical Research Council unit one evening, Sigrid recollected "feeling glad" that Sylvia was the nurse on duty. As they became friends and shared their stories, they found themselves instinctively beginning to care for each other. Life had not been smooth for either of them, and there was a mutual understanding of each other's concerns. However, when Sigrid's stay in Uganda ended, they went their separate ways and lost touch. A few years later, back in Britain, they met up again and over several more years a closer friendship developed and deepened. Neither had sought it—the relationship "just happened." Gradually and joy-fully, they discovered they were in love.

"It was a love that was caring for one another, a love that was about wanting good for the other," said Sylvia. "But there was also an attraction, a wanting to be together." Nevertheless, when it dawned that the friendship was becoming closer, Sigrid swiftly re-treated, initially believing sexual intimacy to be wrong. "Then, at the age of twenty-seven, the penny dropped that my disposition was actually *homosexual*," she said. "I cried when I realized this be-cause I thought my friendship with Sylvia would have to end. But, at the same time, the acknowledgement brought me huge relief be-cause I realized I understood myself and other people much better than I had ever done before."

Sylvia had difficulties of her own at the time. "I didn't struggle with any sense of rightness or wrongness," she told me. "I didn't have any label of sexuality to apply to myself. I just happened to fall in love with Sigrid and to find that love reciprocated. After a time of great uncertainty in my life, I felt that at last I had a sense of belonging, though Sigrid's anxiety placed its own vulnerable edge on that." Sylvia's personal challenge lay in the realm of her deep maternal nature. She knew she would have to forsake the idea of having children if she were to enter into a full relationship with Sigrid. "It seemed as though that choice was being made for me," said Sylvia. "I had met the person I wanted to share my life with."

The women set up home together in Stockport in 1976 and were eager to become part of a local church. One nearby had been recom-mended to them. Although its tradition was Anglican, they instantly felt at home and joined the congregation, still uncertain if their rela-tionship, which they had kept secret, would be acceptable in the eyes of other Christians. At that time they knew of no other homo-sexual people and felt alone. Nonetheless, they took on roles in the church, becoming involved with the Sunday school and missionary-related activities. Members of the congregation, aware that they lived together, would remark that they seemed "just like sisters." But they realized the friendships would not deepen until they disclosed that they were actually partners. They decided to tell a married couple—and to their surprise they found a degree of understanding.

Just before they moved house, to be nearer Sylvia's place of work, they discovered to their sorrow and shame that another member of the congregation had been struggling with his homosexuality all along and they had not known of it. As they settled into their new home in Macclesfield, Sigrid and Sylvia resolved that their relationship should become more transparent. They wanted people to have the freedom to speak with them about matters of sexuality if they felt the need. There would also be a greater integrity on their part if they were invited to lead groups in the church and could be open about themselves. But the couple admit that, because of the prevailing attitude in the church at large toward homosexuals, they had "a rough ride within the relationship and a rough ride outside of it too."

During the early 1980s, Sigrid became seriously depressed. On one occasion, during a Bible study, a parishioner talked about how he had managed to "put away" his gayness, drawing attention to certain biblical passages that had enabled him to overcome his feelings of same-sex attraction. "I remember sitting there and feeling threatened by what I was hearing," Sigrid recalled. "That fed my worries. I withdrew into myself and felt less and less able to be open. I had known a freedom in speaking but now my fear took over."

Sylvia gently guided Sigrid through several dark years. The couple realized how isolated they were in the parish. Though they were accepted and included in many ways, there was no one they could turn to for unequivocal support and encouragement in their relationship. Then Sylvia decided to contact an author who'd written on the subject of homosexuality. He put her in touch with two other women. The veil of a hidden network slowly lifted, much to their surprise and delight. The couple discovered that, while they were becoming preoccupied with whether or not their lifestyle was doctrinally possible, many others throughout the country were facing exactly the same dilemma. Introversion turned to extroversion, uncertainty to confidence, doubt to faith. One morning, as Sigrid was studying her Bible on the commuter train to work, a text from the Gospel of John impelled her toward greater self-exposure. In the passage, Jesus responds to Nicodemus: "For all who do evil hate the light and do not come to the light, so that their deeds may not be exposed. But those who do what is true come to the light, so that it may be clearly seen that their deeds have been done in God" (John 3:20–21).

"That was a turning point for me in the depression and has been a pivotal concept ever since," said Sigrid. "As a result I even wrote a poem which encapsulated what I felt then—and I still own it now. It was about letting something good be seen for what it is. I decided not to retreat again. I can easily slip back into fear but those verses and the poem repeatedly take me out of it again."

The late 1980s were difficult for Sigrid too, but the challenges came from another direction. AIDS was the subject of daily headlines, and harsh pronouncements were being made about the homosexual community. "I remember listening to the news one morning and thinking that if some people's viewpoints were actually carried through, homosexuals would be locked up for the good of society," said Sigrid. "I was shocked and even frightened by the thought that there were those who felt women like us should be incarcerated. I could perceive of its being potentially possible the way the matter was being spoken about with such vehemence. We were dangerous simply because we loved one another. I internalized these negative feelings to such an extent that I once wondered how I dared go to Holy Communion. Then, clearly, I heard in my head the words, 'Because Jesus says, *Come.*' That gave me enormous courage. I realized my faith was deeper than the words being thrown at us."

However, the price of publicly going against the evangelical grain has proved high for both of them. When their local church's ethos changed and became more overtly evangelical, the couple felt increasingly alienated. Sylvia had been permitted to speak at services and plan parish events. But now, under a new regime, people began to regard her with greater suspicion and hostility. She was no longer invited to speak, and her views on any subject were increasingly disregarded. There was a strong sense of "Well, if *she's* saying it, it can't be right." Sylvia remembered voicing an opinion during a church council meeting. The chairperson turned to someone else and asked, "Is she right?" Sylvia commented, "It was only a little phrase but it was such a put down."

They stayed in that church for some time, but the ethos became increasingly destructive and disabling. They knew they had to move for their own sanity and well-being. "Church is supposed to strengthen and resource Christians for their daily lives. Instead, our spirits were being sapped," said Sigrid. "We had obligations to fulfill and creative work to do. We needed to find somewhere that would enable and not threaten our working lives."

Fortunately they found an Anglican church they liked and joined in again with a worshiping community. Sylvia immediately felt a huge sense of belonging and purpose again, becoming part of the teaching, preaching, and worship group. When she spoke at services, people seemed to appreciate her words. Then, overnight, the climate dramatically changed. The bishop was consulted, and she was told she could no longer take any leadership role. The ban followed a sermon she had given on the theme of family values. Eyebrows had started rising when Sylvia's name appeared beside that topic on the weekly preaching rota. Some worshipers believed that, as a person in a homosexual relationship, she was determined to destroy marriage and would speak against family values. Yet the sermon had been entirely in keeping with the tenets of the faith and, in any event, Sylvia had always been much in favor of marriage and committed relationships. "Having spoken in a way which many others judged favorably it was suggested that I was somehow even more dangerous," said Sylvia. Subsequently both women were barred from leadership roles in a church that was always urging its members to use their gifts. But others in the congregation offered support and friendship. However, for the next two years, the pain caused by misrepresentation and a sense of impotence in the face of rejection were almost more than Sylvia could handle. Had it not been for supportive work colleagues as well as a network of gay Christian friends, the situation would have been unbearable, she said.

In 1997, after retiring from the medical world, Sigrid decided she would like to represent the congregation as a member of the ecumenical group Churches Together in Macclesfield. Her creative contributions were initially welcomed, especially as events for the millennium were being planned. She supported the group wholeheartedly, attending all the meetings and offering assistance at every stage. At about the same time, she and Sylvia put an advertisement in the local paper highlighting the fact that gay Christians met at their home and new faces were always welcome. They knew how marginalized gay people could be in small towns. But some members of an independent evangelical church, spotting the small ad, figured out that the Sigrid mentioned in the newspaper was the same Sigrid who participated in the Churches Together group. The discovery ignited thinly disguised prejudices and, like a microcosm of the Jeffrey John affair, there were threats of congregations withdrawing from the Churches Together body because Sigrid was in a committed homosexual partnership. "I had gone into this ecumenical venture because I wanted to help churches be together," she said. "Now I was about to be the cause of a fracture. I could not bear that and I chose to resign."

The sense of rejection had such a psychological impact on Sigrid that, when out and about in Macclesfield, she wondered if someone would recognize and condemn her. It was a time of bewilderment, vulnerability, and fear. "A few years earlier we had spent some time visiting local churches seeing where we might fit," she said. "Now I didn't think I could show my face anywhere because I was this person with a conspicuous label across me. But many individuals offered their support. These are people who still love us, care about us and look out for us."

Sigrid and Sylvia said they were all too aware of how hard it was for lesbian and gay people to hang onto the belief that God loved them when so much of what they kept hearing was about God actively disliking the very people they were. To try to get a different message across, Sigrid and Sylvia felt moved to make a banner for the local millennial March for Jesus. The banner proclaimed, "God is Love not Hate." Sigrid explained, "We carried it through the streets of Macclesfield, although some of the organizers pressured us not to. They objected to the fact that the banner also identified us as 'Christian Lesgays.'" If lesbian and gay people are hearing that they are bad and that they are inherently wrong, Sylvia is not surprised that some of them go off and lead promiscuous lives.

Circumstances have forced the couple to approach life and

matters of faith with a stark honesty, a realism borne of a raw experience of life in the church. "We have not been able to receive hand-me-down answers because they have not been there for us," says Sylvia. "We have had to find the courage to live without them and maybe that's a gift that we can offer." Sigrid thinks that lesbians and gay men bring to the church "a refreshing way of looking at relationships or perhaps a re-invigoration of what a relationship is."

When others fail to recognize the love Sigrid and Sylvia have for each other as *real* love, they find it particularly hard. "For me," said Sigrid, "it is probably the most wounding thing when the love we share is being rubbished and discounted." "And it angers me," Sylvia added, "when people who haven't strained to hear, see or engage with us, who don't know how we structure our lives, who don't know what we mean to each other, just dismiss us by saying 'homosexual relationships are wrong—genital relationships are wrong.'"

For Sigrid and Sylvia, love is all about knowing and being known, warts and all. It is about daring to give and to trust themselves to each other, sharing their lives in their entirety, for good or for ill. "And both the pain and the joy of it," Sigrid explains, "resonate so much with what Christians believe, as well as with what the Bible says about God and God's relationship with humankind. Although some of our experiences in the church have been very bruising, our Christian faith has been deepened, for in and through it all we glimpse God in Jesus standing shoulder to shoulder with us, knowing and feeling exactly what it is for love to be misunderstood and cast aside."

nineteen

Light and Shade

"I hate the darkness," he kept saying, "but I love the light." It was a dank December morning as Christiaan Snyman emerged from the subway station in multi-layered clothing. The opera singer from Johannesburg had flown into London for an audition. But as we roamed through the damp streets of Covent Garden, it was apparent that he was mourning the light and the sun of his native South Africa. Christiaan is also a gifted painter whose homeland has inspired many of his contemporary works of art.

Christiaan's spiritual journey as a young gay man has had its own lugubrious interludes—he once attempted suicide by drinking poison. But now, at the age of thirty, he is deeply in love. During our conversations throughout the day, it was evident that he was missing "the warmth and safety" of his relationship back home. He checked frequently for text messages from his partner. Within minutes of our meeting, he was opening his wallet and showing me a picture of the young man in his life. "There's a lot to be said for a happy relationship," he said. "I have been with this person for eight months—I've never been with anyone that long before. But I had to face a lot of fears at the outset. I was afraid I might not be a committing type of person, as my mind is very free and I get distracted easily. I don't tend to concentrate on any one thing for a long time. But I feel comfortable with this relationship and I feel right with God. You can really give to one person if you love them. It's a wonderful experience of giving and receiving."

Christiaan, whose parents are teachers, grew up as an only child in Klerksdorp, a town in the North West province. Raised in the

Dutch Reformed Church, the state religion of the former apartheid regime, he soon learned what a by-the-book faith was all about. If you were a member of the DRC, people said, it would always look good on your resume. The church offered clear models for men and women. Every man was expected to work and provide for his family. He remembered that, when he was five, his parents would sometimes ask him why they had heard from other children that he was a sissy. He sensed they thought there was something wrong with him. His father was studying child development at the time and might have been suspicious.

"I was always advised that I should be a man," he recalled. "I was encouraged not to make friends with other boys at school who were considered to be different or soft. It was assumed I would play rugby—the big cultural pursuit in South Africa—and cricket. I was actually forced to do rugby but that only lasted a couple of months because they could very clearly see I was useless at it. I carried that failure of masculinity around with me for a very long time. I still struggle with that today. Normally people don't see me as effeminate but I do not feel strongly masculine, which I was brought up to desire."

Christiaan's attraction to men emerged slowly. When he was fourteen, he went into the hospital for a leg operation. On the first night in the ward, another male patient, who was eighteen, made advances on him. That triggered "some kind of fantasy and continued to intrigue me." But the thought that he, too, might actually be homosexual created such a build-up of internal pressure that, from the age of sixteen, he started suffering from acute depression. "My mind was opening up and I was starting to see the world differently," he said. "I began to realize there were opinions to hold other than those of my parents. I was developing sexually and spiritually. It was an emotional awakening.

"But, as a result, I became more secluded and cut myself off from the mainstream macho types. This made me feel very inferior and, even to this day, I struggle with the fact that I have never really felt like a true man. I know that, to God, a real man is someone who loves the Lord passionately against all odds and against his culture—and that takes courage—but I didn't see it that way when I was younger. I felt like an outcast. The guys at school used to tease me and bully me badly. I always lived with a sense of fear because I was always expecting someone to come and beat me up."

Christiaan said that, while he did not understand depression or its emotional depths at the time, he had always experienced it as "the black hole, a duvet, a heavy gray cloak which covered my mind." He lost the ability to act rationally. He even wanted to end his life. At the age of seventeen, he swallowed the organic insecticide he had bought for the orchids he loved to collect. He almost went into a coma. Just before being rushed to the hospital, he found his eyes would no longer focus. "I lost my vision and at the same time was afraid that God might not forgive me for what I had done, so I just asked him to. I think the attempted suicide was directly linked to my being gay. It had been so heavily suppressed because of the culture I lived in."

Even though the Dutch Reformed Church had been notoriously homophobic, Christiaan felt that somehow he had managed to have an experience of Christ while worshiping within it. "But if you have to suppress your sexuality, you cannot develop as a balanced human being with feelings of self-worth," he told me. "This is not surprising if you constantly have a sense of guilt, believe you're in the wrong, think you'll go to hell and feel that you won't be accepted for who you are. But by the grace of God I got through."

After school he joined charismatic churches where he became more zealous and undertook leadership training. There had been "tremendous amounts of unconditional love" coming toward him from God that he had never felt from his parents or teachers. He had needed to share the divine love being bestowed on him. "It flows abundantly. But you have to be a channel as well; otherwise you block the light and it becomes dark."

With his flowing, dark brown hair, intensity of expression, and spiritual insights, Christiaan reminded me of a modern-day mystic. I was therefore not entirely surprised to learn that out of profound feelings of unworthiness had emerged a series of impassioned spiritual experiences where he had felt warmth, love, and a reassurance within the depths of his soul. A voice had continually said to him, "I love you. I love you. I care for you. I will get you through this."

He thought this meant he would become straight. But that didn't happen. He reached a point when he felt he was living by faith alone. He couldn't go back to the church because he would have been judged, even though he needed spiritual sustenance. The support from friends was insufficient, and he couldn't count on the understanding of his parents because he did not feel, at that stage, that it was appropriate to disclose the truth about himself. So he had God alone to rely on and he was clinging to his faith. "I remember very clearly in 2001 lying on my bed and saying to God, 'Well, I can't take this pressure any more. Whether you like this or not, I cannot go on as I am. I do not want to be a Christian any more. I cannot stand it. These people who preach love judge me without love but I would love to be like Christ. I want to love him and obey him. I know that I love Christ and I identify with him. I know he went through a lot of suffering and, like me, was alone.' In speaking to God in that way, I felt a release. A spiritual mother later told me to stay close to God and not to worry about religion because that was man-made."

In recent years Christiaan has drifted from institutional religion. He said he felt guilty about not going to services, but he could never be a member of a church which condemned who he was. His new relationship, meanwhile, has actually resulted in his "spending more time with God." He told me, "Being in relationship with a guy who has the same feeling toward God, a similar spiritual outlook and is also sensitive made me feel I had come home. Within that safety, I have been able to approach God again and trust that he has been carrying the relationship. I am not angry any more. I think being gay has made me humble and kept me close to God. Perhaps if I had been a very masculine, run-of-the-mill type of guy in my culture, I would not really have needed God because I would have been able to rely on myself more. In South African culture, men are not encouraged to have close male friends. They have the rugby, the beer and the camaraderie."

Christiaan's mystical approach to life and eternity is reflected particularly in his work as an artist. It mirrors his struggles and his faith. He described himself as an "extremely emotional person" and said that characteristic was often unveiled through his pictures. "I don't always understand myself, so I don't always know what is taking place on the canvas," he commented. "I also get these moments when I feel I am actually falling into the passion of doing it. It's as if my mind goes into a different gear altogether. It's a spiritual experience. You could say I go into a trance. I fall flat on my face and pray. Everything becomes silent within me. It's as if I go deeper then. I feel reassured and safe. Then I find I can really pray deeply. When I'm painting away I always go into that very deep place. It's not like smoking a joint because I am totally in my mind and I feel energized.

"I feel alive when I paint. I feel whole as a being, as I do when I sing. I could never take discipline as a child, whereas in my singing and in my art I am naturally disciplined. I'm always talking to God when I'm painting and while I am singing, whether I am struggling in my life or feeling elated. That is my worship. That is my service to God because I feel an intimacy with him when I create. I feel safe within that energy and I feel connected with him. Sexually as well there is a certain kind of energy when you love someone that way. That same gut energy emerges when I paint or sing. I think art helps me wrestle with all these personal issues of faith and sexuality—and then singing releases the burden."

twenty

Master of Disguise

Growing up as a gay or lesbian person presents its challenges in any locality. But in Northern Ireland, where conservative views on homosexuality are so deeply embedded in both the Protestant and Catholic communities, coming to terms with your deepest self can take a lifetime. For many gay people there, the mask of marriage is often the most effective form of disguise.

According to the president of Northern Ireland's Gay Rights Association, between eighty and ninety percent of Northern Ireland's wider gay community are married with families. "These men are so used to telling lies, even to themselves, they now can't think straight," said P. A. MagLochlainn, a Catholic teacher turned gay activist, as he relaxed in a chic Belfast café wearing a "Pride" T-shirt. "They wed because of the guidance they once received from a pastor, priest, doctor or psychiatrist who meant well but advised, 'Forget about this oul' carry on. Get yourself a girlfriend, and it will be all right.' But it was not all right, and consequently these men are now leading double lives."

Ironically, the only march in Northern Ireland where Catholics and Protestants walk together is the annual Gay Pride "Dander," where gay and straight people from different traditions not only move in unison, but even hold hands. "It's the final, climactic event of our annual Gay Pride week here in Belfast," he said. "It is widely recognized as the most colorful and happiest parade in the calendar, and it's attracting more and more visitors every year." In Northern Ireland, homosexuality has at times proved to be a greater binding force than religion. While churches in the province are still set apart, the gay community has long made an ecumenical impact. Protestants and Catholics who secretly live together in gay and lesbian relationships tend to be spared the stigmatization weathered by some couples in mixed marriages.

A keen supporter of the nationalist Social Democratic and Labor Party, MagLochlainn became the first openly gay person to be elected to the central executive committee of any political party in the United Kingdom or the Republic of Ireland. But such a profile was unimaginable when he was growing up at the height of the Troubles. Educated in a minor seminary, which taught the Catholic faith "in great detail," he later read Scholastic Philosophy as part of his degree at Queen's University, Belfast. "Having studied church history, rubrics, apologetics and so on, I learned about everything from Thomas Aquinas to Kierkegaard, and from logic to eastern mysticism. One of my lecturers later became Cardinal Primate of all Ireland. All the time, I was evaluating all this learning and teaching against a secret awareness of my own sexuality."

It was at university that the young MagLochlainn first read a book about homosexuality. "You've no idea what a breakthrough this was for me," he said. "Until then I had found absolutely nothing except the usual biblical texts, which I'd already begun to evaluate critically. And just as I saw that Aquinas' much-touted *Proofs for the Existence of God* were not in fact proofs at all, so too did I realize that the traditional scriptural 'evidence' condemning homosexuality was largely human misinterpretation." He remembered devouring a book, *Homosexuality*, by D. J. West, and rereading it. "But it was so uninspiring, dismaying and dispiriting that, without thinking what I was doing, I took a vow of celibacy so I could forget about that side of me. I retreated and deliberately grew a beard because I did not want to be a fresh-faced youth any more or to be in any intimate contact with other people."

So, with a degree in French, he went into teaching and taught in two schools, eventually joining the staff of the Christian Brothers' grammar school in Omagh. For the next twenty years he "sublimated like mad" and, away from the classroom, "got involved in everything," a classic characteristic of homosexual suppression. "I became a committee person, often serving as secretary," he said.

Joining the nascent Social Democratic and Labor Party (SDLP), he became a founder member of the Omagh branch. He gave a series of lectures with the Workers' Education Association (which led to the setting up of Omagh Family History Group), helped found and run Omagh's Life-Saving Club, organized chess tournaments, and appeared on stage in many serious roles. "But my greatest successes were in pantomime," he recalled fondly. "I was an absolutely odious villain—and always copped it in the last act with a most realistic pratfall. The children usually howled with glee!"

An ever-present fear, however, was that another man might sense his sexuality and take an amorous interest in him. He did not want to be attractive to anyone. So he grew his beard long, black, and luxuriant. As the Irish playwright George Bernard Shaw reportedly put it, "I grew my beard out of a young man's foolish pride and I kept it on through common sense." MagLochlainn further camouflaged his true self by growing his hair long, wearing horn-rimmed spectacles, and donning a tweed jacket and corduroy trousers. He said that people who knew him these days would probably find it impossible to identify him in photographs from that period.

"I was kidding myself when I was the man with the beard, thinking I was one thing while actually being another," he told me. "One part of me was in full disguise, hiding who I really was. Toward the end of his life, the English Jesuit poet Gerald Manley Hopkins said something about drying up and praying for God to send his roots rain. It was like that for me. I was turning into a proper little 'schoolmarm.' I had entirely stopped reading poetry; my whole study now was history. I was forgetting about feelings and becoming more and more exact, pedantic and dry. I was turning myself into a machine."

But many years later, after a spontaneous relationship at the age of forty-three, and a near-death experience while sailing off the west coast of Ireland, he found himself totally reassessing his life. And that was when he finally decided to come out. This inevitably meant leaving his teaching job, so he planned a new future in information technology. He decided to shave off his beard, changing in both appearance and attitude almost overnight. It was a complete about-turn, the outward signs of an inner transformation. His plans for a new career in computers, however, were overtaken by ill health, which forced him into early retirement. By now he was devouring everything he could read about homosexuality and drifting into gay activism.

"I got rid of all the teacher gear, put on jeans, abandoned the glasses and bought contact lenses," he revealed. "Then I had a crew-cut. I walked up and down Omagh main street talking to friends who had no idea who I was. It was a complete change of identity. My mental well-being improved. I became more positive. My mother said she had never seen me look so healthy. I think I will live longer than I might otherwise have done because now I am free of stress. I didn't think I would ever have a relationship because I'm no particular catch. I had buried myself in my work as a habit. But later I found a partner, a Protestant, and our relationship lasted for eight-and-a-half glorious years. I regard those years as a bonus, a grace, a gift from God to a rather unworthy individual, who is still rather ashamed that it took him so long to face down the world and tell the truth about the way God had made him. For I am certain that God made me gay—and meant me to be gay.

"I think our whole attitude in the gay community to relationships has much to teach the heterosexual community. We have almost completely abandoned the notion of power relationships within partnerships, and view friendship as a gift. No one 'owns' anyone else any more. A good relationship is one that allows and encourages both partners to grow into better versions of themselves. And if a partnership reaches its end, this is not necessarily either partner's fault: we should look honestly to what is best for our loved one, and accept whatever this entails. All love is a reflection (no matter how dim) of the divine love."

For all his use of theological language, MagLochlainn describes himself as an atheist. But he says he still tries to live by Christian principles, describing them wryly as "as good an ethic as you could get." Organized religion has not served gay people well, he insists. Although he had been hurt by the church in the past, he did not "necessarily blame" the institution whose priests spoke with the wisdom they had had at the time. But in the event of the last judgment, he thought he would take his chances with Christ because "Christ has never said anything that would make me afraid." Conversely, he would be "very afraid" of any judgment meted out by "all too many of Christ's so-called Christian interpreters." God did not make mistakes, he said. God "clearly made some of us gay." Gay people were no more fallen than anyone else. Christ had not referred to homosexuality, yet some Christians "would have us believe it a 'crime' worse than murder. Christ is very clear about murder or child abuse but he never once mentions homosexuality."

Coming out in his early forties gave MagLochlainn a sense of wholeness. He felt free to live his life at last, and stopped looking over his shoulder. He always used to speculate why so many spies, like Burgess and MacClean, were gay. He speculated on whether it was simply because leading a double life became so natural. MagLochlainn said the energy he had used up trying to deceive people into thinking he was heterosexual had been "wasted effort." It was strange indeed, he reflected, how many people spent all their time discriminating against gay people, obsessively looking for and punishing any hint of homosexuality in their neighbor, while many others wasted as much energy in hiding it, when they could both be putting all that energy to better use for the whole community.

MagLochlainn, who became president of Northern Ireland's Gay Rights Association in 1991, accepted that many people in the gay community had become over-politicized and under-spiritualized, but suggested that was probably the sour fruit of rejection. There were still churches in Northern Ireland which were fiercely anti-gay and cruel in their attitude to young gay people, he pointed out. "If you come out as a homosexual, you are cut off from your family completely. You are abandoned. You are un-personed. Young gay teens there are up to six times more likely to commit suicide as their straight peers."

In Northern Ireland, the Roman Catholic Church directly controls over half the schools while the Protestant churches have special rights in most others. Northern Ireland's schools officially have no gay pupils. "Not a single school mentions sexual orientation in its literature, let alone how it aspires to enable gay children to develop into normal gay adults," MagLochlainn explained. "The whole Northern Ireland educational establishment would have us believe that gay people here appear overnight at the age of eighteen, like button mushrooms in fairy circles on the lawn. Where do gay teenagers turn? The gay teenager is uniquely lonely and isolated, especially in Northern Ireland. Were she black or Jewish, she would be supported by her black or Jewish family. If disabled, society at large would at least pay lip service to helping her. Teachers are swift to stop other children from name-calling or bullying black, Jewish or disabled pupils. Yet some of these same teachers not only connive at but lead the oppression of their gay pupils.

"All our experience shows that the greatest single factor in dissipating homophobia is knowing and respecting someone gay. That is why the early gay rights activists always held that if all the gay people in society came out, this would banish homophobia overnight. There is something undeniable and unmistakable about truth and sincerity.

"A closet is a wardrobe. You can't achieve anything inside a wardrobe. You run out of air and starve yourself of light. It is not a place to develop anything. Any plant that grows in a wardrobe emerges as a pale shadow of itself. Gay people have to live in the full ray of the sun, in the fullness of truth, as much as they possibly can."

twenty-one

Out of the Wilderness

If the Diocese of New Hampshire had not elected Gene Robinson as the first openly gay bishop in the Anglican Communion, it might well have selected a lesbian priest instead. The Rev. Dr. Bonnie Ring was one of the other nominees. With an entry in *Who's Who in the West*, Bonnie Ring had an enviable track record in social justice work and psychology. During the 1960s, she had participated in the student rights movement and knew Martin Luther King Jr. personally. She was a counseling psychologist at the University of California during the 1970s and, before training to be a priest in the 1980s, she presented her own daily psychological call-in show on a radio station.

"Applying for the New Hampshire post had nothing to do with my sexuality," said Bonnie, who is sixty-three. "It was about my wanting to be the pastor of a small diocese in a part of the United States I have loved since I was a child. Everybody who knew me told me to go for it. I put my heart and soul into the application which made me realize that I could be a bishop, even though this had never been part of my self-expectations." With the application form came a list of "fabulous questions," which offered opportunities for Bonnie to describe her real-life saints, the people who had influenced her and the vision she had for the church.

But almost immediately she realized the possible consequences for her eleven-year relationship with the Rev. Terri Grotzinger, herself an Episcopal priest. "We had to look at how taking up the post might change our lives and we had to talk about what Terri might have to surrender in the process," Bonnie explained. "I do not think I could have responded to the uproar that ensued with the grace that Gene has because I dislike overt conflict. I think he had the advantage of being almost a native son. They had known him for twenty years. They loved him. They trusted him. I am very glad it didn't happen to me and I am very glad it did happen to him."

Bonnie recalled how, a quarter of a century before, she had been sitting with a gay bishop who was frightened of declaring his true colors. She had heard the aching of his heart because he could not be open. She had seen him die of alcoholism because he was so torn. Now, twenty-five years later, it was exciting to be in the Diocese of California, where people had been authorized to address the questions of homosexuality in the context of tradition, experience, and reason. It was staggering to realize that what could not have been mentioned in public in the late 1970s was now something everyone was talking about. Following the Lambeth Resolution of 1998, which stated that homosexuality was incompatible with Scripture, Bonnie chaired a task force, sponsored by the Bishop of California, which addressed the issues raised at Lambeth and challenged them on the basis of the primary commandment to love God and neighbor. "We are all at different levels of readiness but the Spirit is at work," she said.

One of the most wonderful encounters to come Bonnie's way since the election of Gene Robinson was a visit from a psychotherapy client, a practicing Buddhist, who told her that he and his teenage son had both decided that, if ever they chose to experience Christianity in the future, it would have to be through the Episcopal Church because they were so proud of the stance it had taken. But Bonnie also accepted that, for every positive reaction she received, somebody else might well be horrified. She did not feel compelled to stand up in front of every congregation and proclaim that she was a lesbian. "I am just so proud of our church that they would take a man they knew and loved, disregard his sexuality and vote him in as their bishop," she said. "That is what I yearn for: that what we do sexually, or what our color or nationality are, shouldn't matter."

Terri, meanwhile, was impressed by the way in which General Convention had been openly discussing the issue of homosexuality for many years. At the 2003 convention, people had listened carefully and had then decided to vote with their consciences. It had been a "massive breakthrough" for Terri to see a high school student standing up during live television coverage of the convention debate and stating why she believed it was appropriate to affirm Gene Robinson. This had resulted in conversations that could not have happened five years before. A broad spectrum of influential figures in the church had clearly believed that the decision was the will of God. Now they all needed to move on and Terri found herself facing a new priestly challenge. "It's now my responsibility as a priest in the church to help that message be heard and received, just like anything else which emerges from General Convention," she pointed out. "It's no longer just my issue or our issue, a small community's issue or a particular church's issue. It is something I have even greater responsibility to speak to now."

Bonnie, who hails from New York, grew up in a nominally Jewish family. She became a Christian at the age of fourteen and later an Episcopalian. She moved to the West Coast when she was twenty-five and remained there. Describing herself as "a late-blooming lesbian," she explained that she had lived as a heterosexual woman until she fell in love with Terri. "I married more than once but never had children. I kept looking for the right relationship that would meet all the social expectations of a professional woman. I learned how to get out of my marriages and, as homosexually friendly as I was, I never considered that I might be lesbian."

The couple met at Berkeley through a mutual friend while Terri was studying at the Church Divinity School of the Pacific. Bonnie had already finished her seminary training there and was working as a teacher, therapist, and spiritual director. She was ordained priest in December 1992 at the age of fifty-two. Five weeks later she entered the relationship with Terri. "I wrestled with God all night long," she recalled. "I remember acknowledging to God on the day of my ordination that I had been avoiding relationships but, if it was God's will that I be in one, then I would be open to it. When I realized I had sexual feelings for Terri, I said to God that that was not the kind of relationship I had meant. But God just didn't let up. There was no out. I didn't stop and think about the consequences. I trusted my feelings. I'd had many years of therapy. It felt right and I couldn't explain it.

"As a one-time Jew, I had felt like an outcast in many ways since adolescence. It took my becoming a lesbian to realize that I shouldn't expect my priesthood to be any different. I was on the margins. I have had to live from that place and it's perfectly logical that I carry all of that into the priesthood and use it fruitfully."

Terri was raised in California. She was a member of both the Methodist and Presbyterian traditions before becoming an Episcopalian at the age of thirty-one. Until she had concretely owned the truth of herself as a lesbian woman, matters of authenticity and integrity kept emerging as she pondered her priestly vocation. "If God calls you to something, then your wholeness is going to keep getting called out of you," she said. During the ordination selection procedure, nobody quizzed Terri directly about her sexuality. During the psychological evaluations, she discussed her call to priesthood and the exploration of her sexuality. She was reassured that she was asking the right kind of questions. It was suggested that she should keep following her spiritual instincts and not feel discomfited.

"I had been in other lesbian relationships yet had always wondered what God might be calling me to. But the relationship with Bonnie felt different," she told me. "In fact, it felt right, even though I was about to graduate and become a priest. I knew I wanted to go forward with both. If you are going to be whole, you have to own the person you are. You have to do that at all levels. The idea that I would somehow know I was lesbian but then have to bury it somewhere didn't work for me. Like Lazarus I had to step out of that tomb."

Terri originally worked as a wildlife biologist and resource manager. Serving in the U.S. Department of Agriculture Forest Service near Yellowstone, Montana, and in the Bob Marshall Wilderness near Glacier National Park, Terri believed her vocation lay as a "wilderness person." Indeed, this remains part of her deepest calling, for it was in the great outdoors that she learned not only about ecology but about relationships and the marginalized of creation. "In the wilderness, it's all about relationships. I was dealing with the habitats of threatened and endangered species such as grizzly bears, bald eagles and peregrine falcons. By the time I started looking at my own sexuality and my priesthood, I realized there was a connection. I could relate to my own journey because I was dealing with it in the context of wider creation. The experience has made me much more open to all kinds of different people whom I may not understand but who end up being marginalized because those in the majority decide what happens."

Today, at Holy Family Episcopal Church, Half Moon Bay, on the Pacific coast, the forty-six-year-old serves a community which accepts her as a lesbian in a committed relationship. In fact, before Terri was appointed, the parish invited Bonnie along to the interview. Members of the congregation always ask about Bonnie and make her feel welcome whenever they see her. The couple share a home seven miles away. They sometimes attend parish events together. Bonnie occasionally assists in the parish but her ministry is chiefly that of spiritual direction, retreat work and psychotherapy for clergy and seminarians. She is also employed part-time as the interim associate of a parish in Oakland. "To a large extent, because I am older, with educational qualifications and a lot of professional experience, as well as being a lesbian, I haven't been very employable," she admitted. "I have had to make my own living by doing and discovering ministry. I was turned down for a lot for jobs, so I stopped applying for them."

It took Bonnie six years to become a priest. Her bishop had many reservations because she had been a liberal political activist, involved in Christian social justice programs including inter-racial mission work. She was instrumental in founding the Episcopal Society for Cultural and Racial Unity, which led to her involvement in the civil rights movement. "The bishop thought I was a little too self-righteous," she smiled. "One of the things I learned in the civil rights movement, mainly from Martin Luther King Jr., is that God created all of us and God doesn't make junk. There have always been people who were acceptable to society and people who were rejected in different ages through history for different reasons. But God can use anybody, taking people whom the culture or institution deem unacceptable and ensuring they are included as part of God's creation. I think God calls all of us to wrap our arms around all kinds of people."

Bonnie said there had been division in the Episcopal Church of

North America for more than thirty years over civil rights, the ordination of women and contemporary language in the prayer book. Now it was the turn of homosexuality. "In many ways the conservatives have held us hostage, always threatening to leave and therefore getting us to mollify and do nothing to threaten union," she said. "I don't think most Episcopalians worry about the Anglican Communion as though their lives and religion depended on it. Every church should have to have a gay or lesbian nominee for their rector, just so they go through the issues of what the Gospel calls them to and what it will cost them."

For Terri, being in a relationship has enhanced her priesthood through the fearless living out of the love she and Bonnie have for one another. They now encourage others to live more openly. "I believe the Gospel causes someone somewhere to step forth and, every time that happens, that stepping out of the tomb like Lazarus changes the world," she said. "Some of those watching will fight it. Some will want it. Some will be afraid of how to reach out to it. But God does that over and over again. Scripture is full of such examples. It's not that we're abandoning Scripture. Moreover, Scripture is part of why we do what we do. The idea that my life is lived out first as a lesbian person and then as a Christian is back to front. It was Scripture, my fellow Christians and their prayers that helped me know who I was as a lesbian woman. This drew me out of my own tomb and enabled me to trust in my sexuality.

"I am not going to give up who I am in God's eyes. If I am wrong, God will reckon that. But there's too much peace in it and too much willingness to step out again and again. I hope that what we do will enable change to occur elsewhere; that some ripple effect, some encouragement, some grace falls from it for others. Hopefully, with my ability to reach between, to be a bridge, I bring a welcome, an openness to people and a willingness to listen to different perspectives. This is the place where I get in touch with those who have no voice. I have to be open to all of those conversations to know what it is like to be too scared to be out; to have questions and not be able to get the answers you want quickly; and to realize that, once you step forth, there is no going back. That is true of all our spiritual journeys."

twenty-two

The Inner Voice of Truth

Tim Pike entered his parents' room calmly. They said nothing but were noticeably tearful. Their son was all in black, except for the little white square over his throat. That was the first time they had seen him in a collar. As other guests, including his sister's family, started to arrive, Tim began to feel nervous, even though there was little for him to do at the Mass except stand up with a few other seminarians and say "present." After five years' training, they were about to be recognized officially as candidates for the priesthood. Ordination was still some way off.

That day Tim found himself listening with particular care to the bishop's homily. He was preaching about how sin could cause disintegration "from the inside of a person as well as inside a community." Those words lingered. "I didn't know that the lies within *me* were crippling," Tim explained, "and that, within a week, I would be crumbling so much inside myself that I would have to seek some guidance. Yet, for all that, it was a good day. I felt proud and I held my head high."

That afternoon, in his freshly pressed clerical attire, Tim walked down the local street to be greeted by a succession of stares and a burst of "Hello Vicar!" He averted his eyes, trying to look as relaxed and as natural as possible. But it was all pretense. "In reality," he admitted, "it was a relief when I took off the collar and slipped back into my jeans. Within days, waves of inner panic were making me tremble and bringing tears to my eyes."

A week later, Tim began to sense "a well of shame within" and gingerly sought help to confront it. Sympathizing with his emotional turmoil and its implications for his academic deadlines, Tim's tutor listened patiently as the student struggled to articulate "feelings of disgrace that appeared to belong nowhere." He encouraged Tim to return each week to examine his emotions in greater depth. But every time he went back, he dreaded hearing a voice that told him to "keep the doors open" or not to draw "any early conclusions." At most, he had wanted the tutor, a Catholic priest, to accept the fact that there might be some grayness in the area of his sexuality. Then he could leave it there. Or so he thought. But, as the weeks passed, so the "penny dropped deeper into the well" and, gradually, Tim began to "glow with confidence at the shocking news" that he was in fact gay. In the brutally honest self-discernment process that followed, he even found himself reflecting on his own prejudices toward gay men that had been lurking just beneath the surface. "I thought I was gay-friendly but I realized I wasn't," he said. "I considered gay men to be of a lower status: what they did was disgusting. So I had to break through those barriers before I could even begin to look at myself. But, overall, working out that I was gay came as an enormous relief. It was like a huge weight being lifted off my shoulders, even though I hadn't known that burden was there. Everything within me fell into place. It made a lot of sense and felt right."

But informing the seminary and diocesan staff that he wanted to delay his ordination proved unnerving. However, as he stuttered the news to his bishop on the telephone, with his eyes shut tightly, he heard a firm but gentle voice saying to him, "I support you. You have all the time you need." Looking Tim in the eye at a later meeting, the bishop was even more reassuring. "It's wonderful what's happening to you," he said. Such sensitive support, even delight, by senior clerics stood out in striking contrast to the dry official teaching of the church, which, Tim felt, disseminated "suspicion, disgust, guilt, fear and anger." The "divine disclosure" had occurred at a place and a time when he could handle it. If it had happened earlier, the self-loathing, panic, and dread might have proved overwhelming.

For a few weeks at least, Tim appeared to have the best of both worlds. He had come out to himself and some of the staff, but had not yet given up the training. A stifling security and an energizing insecurity competed within him. Tim decided to give himself "permission to experiment" before reaching a final decision about his future. Better, he ruminated, to be put in touch with his "authentic self" now than after his ordination, when temptations might be more risk-laden. He did not want to bring dishonor on the church. So Tim explored his sexuality without inhibition. On one occasion he met a man in a swimming pool and went back to his home. The following day he visited a gay bar, trembling with "an interior cocktail of thrill, amusement, fear and contempt." It seemed dark and grubby, yet thrillingly seductive. He remembered how he had stood beside a wall gulping pints of soda water because he hadn't wanted to distort his senses with anything stronger. "It was all in the eye contact," he revealed. "It was easy to encounter handsome, intelligent men with such little effort. I loved sharing our life stories and feeling loved. But I soon learned about the disappointment too. After promises of a second encounter, there were the unreturned phone calls. I felt used and deceived, cheap and naive. I realized I wasn't loved at all."

Four months later, Tim was flattered to be asked to read at the very Mass at which he would have been ordained deacon. He helped organize the music, the lessons, guests, and photography. It seemed sad, though, to be standing there only as a guest, "but they still let me wear the clerical alb." The cathedral was full. Hundreds of faces looked back at him as he calmly and confidently proclaimed the Word. He loved conveying the meaning of the sacred texts with an appropriate solemnity. But while the pauses, eye contact, and vocal modulations all harmonized that day, his mind was elsewhere.

The previous evening he had been in bed with a lover. "We laughed at the irony of what might have been," Tim explained. "I needed to be with him that night to be certain of what I was choosing and what I was declining. He confirmed me in my decision to hold back from ordination. I knew I needed to explore who I was sexually as a gay man before I could make any decisions about choosing a celibate life."

The ordination ceremony itself provided added reassurance. Tim felt he was making the correct decision. He would never have been able to make the promises with total integrity. He was at peace with the new direction his life was taking, even though many questions persisted, such as "Where is God leading me? Why has he led me this particular way?" For there was no denying the fact that it was an identity he least desired. And he knew himself to be too immature as a gay person to make serious, long-term commitments to any man he met.

The seminary rector had suggested several times that it might be best for Tim to live away from college as he contemplated his future and completed the last months of his theology degree. But Tim had resisted, preferring to keep his head down, finish the course, and "then scuttle off." There was also the feeling that living away from "Mother" would be too daunting a prospect. It suddenly dawned on Tim how totally institutionalized he had become. For six years he had experienced all-male community living—studying, meals, socializing, and worship. Everything had been communal, except a small bedroom that was his own private world. He didn't have a job, car, partner, or bills—just a little pocket money. Tutors, spiritual directors, advisers, and confessors had become the parental figures of a perpetual, early adolescent lifestyle that returned him to a routine of constant dependency. He felt like a thirteen-year-old. At times he was resentful, trapped, and angry yet at the same time always afraid of being expelled from a regime which bred infantility. Tim had previously lived independently for an entire decade with jobs, cars, girlfriends, and a mortgage. Yet here he was, at the age of thirty-two, feeling scared about the prospect of surviving on his own.

Eventually Tim found his own place. Even then, the church remained generous, supporting him with rent, course fees, money for food, and independent counseling. When both the degree and the monetary support were about to end, Tim paid the bishop a visit to thank him for his generosity. He also told him how guilt-laden he felt about all the church had invested in him. "We don't measure things like that," replied the bishop. "Some get ordained. Some don't."

Tim felt the years of formation had not been wasted. It had been "life-giving" and had led to "human freedom." As a support for his future journey, he asked the bishop for a blessing. "I knew

I wouldn't have his hands placed upon my head for ordination, so this simple act was important to me," he reflected. "The bishop stood beside me, placed his hands gently on my head and prayed aloud. He asked the Spirit to guide and protect me. Then he walked me to the front door and opened it. After almost six years, I was walking away from my bishop—and from my ordination. Yet, in that same moment, I felt affirmed, supported and blessed by the church itself. I had become a new man, sanctified by a long process of human, emotional, intellectual and spiritual conversion that had disclosed a self-identity I knew to be created by God. The truth was setting me free and God was doing it in his own time. Gently and firmly the Spirit seemed to be guiding me on a journey toward my authentic personhood. The result has been someone who has been able to be generous, kind, forgiving and patient toward myself, the church and God."

During his first year "out in the church," Tim grew in self-confidence and developed gay friendships. His prayer life seemed to flourish more than it had in the seminary. A simplified form proved more enriching. There remained a sense of divine guidance, purpose, and direction. In a conversation with him at the time, I wondered how he could still live alongside a community which, as he put it, "tenderly authenticated a new identity," yet also taught that, in some sense, he was disordered? "Well, simply by the patience, generosity, kindness and forgiveness I have witnessed and experienced within it," he responded. "It is through a few people in the church that I have learned about these qualities and therefore I, too, feel able to be patient and generous toward the very institution which teaches, on the one hand, that I am in some way flawed and, on the other, that I must also forgive."

When we resumed our conversation two years later, Tim was living in a different part of Britain, qualified in his new profession, out to his colleagues and in a relationship with one of them. "Jon and I are planning a life together," he told me with a broad smile. "Some of the best times we have together are in prayer. We flick through a book by Anthony de Mello and often find a meditation requiring the use of the imagination. At the end of those prayers, I thank God for his generosity to me in every way."

But Tim also pointed out that, because he had found his local Roman Catholic community to be "dry and impersonal," he now worshiped with Jon at an Anglican cathedral. "Jon has been confirmed as an Anglican and I, too, am feeling at home in that tradition," he said. "During the Sunday Eucharist, there are regular prayers that mention support for gay people. Jon and I kiss at the sign of peace. Others must know we are gay. They always make a point of welcoming us. Now I feel open to considering a calling to the priesthood in the Anglican tradition, so long as I can keep my integrity and openness about who I am and who my partner is. This is at the heart of the inner voice of truth.

"I can actually envisage myself as a small bridge between the two traditions. I respect the Anglican Communion for its open, if heated, debates about the morality of monogamous gay relationships. Discussions in the Catholic Church go on too, but always behind closed doors and shrouded in fear. For me, the final straw came when the Holy See issued statements firmly opposing any legal recognition of gay couples. Sadly that has colored my view of all Catholic communities and accounts for the fact that, week by week, I am feeling more at home in the Anglican world, however divided that world may be."

twenty-three

The Long Search

"Being brought up as a fundamentalist Christian seems to have influenced my search for a partner," conceded thirty-two-year-old Davey Gerhard as he bit into his blueberry muffin. "I think I have put rather strict preferences on who I'm looking for, what I will find and what I want when I've found it."

We were having Saturday morning brunch at a gay café in San Francisco, close to Davey's home in the Castro. "I'm the product of a right-and-wrong, yes-and-no brand of Christianity which, as a gay man, has been damaging to me and to others. I have hurt many boyfriends along the way because of that. The longest relationship I've been in here was with a guy on whom I'd imposed my thinking of how it should work. We were going to be immediate, monogamous and intimate, sharing everything with each other. But it was really control on my part."

Davey acknowledged that the city's gay community could, in its own way, be equally fundamentalist. "Life revolves around fetishes here—what you are into," he smiled. "Because I am a big man with a furry face (he weighs about 250 pounds and has a reddish brown beard) they think I must be into other big men with furry faces. Conversations don't run much deeper than that. It's a different form of exclusivity and judgment. Big guys don't talk to thin guys. Asians don't mix with Hispanics. These inward-looking attitudes are so very homogenous. I feel alienated because I like to think of myself as being beyond some of those labels and yet, like many others, I can wear them when I need to."

He grew up in a suburb of Detroit where his family were members of the fundamentalist Church of Christ, one of the starkest forms of Protestantism. Even the playing of musical instruments was forbidden. But it was a place his parents felt compelled to attend twice on Sundays, once on Wednesdays and whenever group meetings were scheduled. Church membership, obligatory attendance and family values were ingrained and interconnected. All Davey heard week by week was why he needed to be saved. Sermons concentrated on "the sinful nature of mankind," constant vigilance against Satan and the need to be reconciled to Christ.

So, as an only child, Davey lived a life of strict religious observance, sitting obediently in the pew alongside his parents and grandparents. But one day when he was twelve, he scribbled a note in his journal which would have profound consequences. "I think I might be slightly homosexual," it said. Davey had found himself attracted to a schoolmate and, as an intelligent pupil, had tried to rationalize his emotions, initiating camouflaged chats with members of the church congregation about the fact that he might never marry. They tried to cast aside his uncertainties. Having known him since birth, he could be nothing other than what they believed and desired him to be. Any acknowledgment of a homosexual inclination would have been denounced as lustful and sinful.

Davey was a member of the youth group but never felt completely at home there. "I'd realized from other experiences that if you didn't behave normally you were quickly blacklisted," he said. "I knew both from my family obligations and my personal desire to be popular that I could never trust anyone enough to reveal anything I might be feeling. The family values in my house were to look normal, be normal, say nothing that would cause any suspicion—and lie if you had to. This was to make certain we were always good Christians."

When Davey's father lost his job, therefore, not a word was uttered to church friends in case it reflected badly on the family. Dirty laundry was always kept firmly in the closet. Davey remembered how, during services, some members of the congregation facing personal difficulties (such as divorce or financial bankruptcy) would come up to the altar in tears, begging forgiveness. They would be prayed over and encouraged positively in public. But in the parking lot afterward, there would be gossip about how Satan had grabbed them and how it wasn't appropriate to associate with them any longer.

Davey said his childhood memories were embedded in the routine of "piling into the car and going to church together." At home, the family said grace at meals and conversed earnestly about God's will but they never prayed or read together. "That was a very lonely time for me. I had no one to talk to about what I really wanted to feel and what I was really thinking about, except on Easter Sundays when my father's parents, who were Episcopalian, came to visit from another state. I was allowed to go to service with them until I was baptized in our church. So once a year I got the greatest and best day of the Christian calendar in the Episcopal Church and the rest of the time I attended this soulless and joyless community. When I was at the Episcopal church with my grandparents, I felt free, sang loudly, participated fully, even though I didn't know all the liturgical actions. I received Holy Communion before I was even baptized."

He remembered, in particular, his mother having a conversation with him when he was fifteen. She was making sure he knew the difference between right and wrong. If he didn't receive full immersion baptism as a personal choice, he would spend eternity in hell. At his mother's insistence one Wednesday evening, Davey gingerly walked out into the aisle during the final hymn. He was welcomed by the preacher and confessed Jesus as his Lord and Savior. He then donned a white robe and was baptized. When he came up out of the water, walked back down the aisle and put his clothes back on, somebody came up and shook his hand. "Congratulations, you have just made the most important decision of your life. Welcome," said the worshiper. Davey thought to himself, "I'm only fifteen years old. How could this be the most important decision of my life? I don't feel any different." He immediately realized nothing had changed. He was still the same person he had always been. Baptism was supposed to have washed away all his sins and given him a clean slate. "But I knew I was still homosexual," he said. "The guy I had a crush on was still sitting in the class—and I still had a crush on him after my baptism. Nothing had changed but I had supposedly made the most important decision of my life."

As the homosexual feelings persisted, Davey began to suspect that their root was much more profound and complex than he had originally assumed. They could not be easily dismissed. This was who he really was. Then his Episcopalian grandmother died and, without her spiritual support, Davey entered a deeper level of loneliness. The local preacher noticed how he had become withdrawn and quizzed him about his grandmother. He told Davey that it must be terrible for him to know that she was in hell because she had not been saved. "That was the last straw," Davey told me. "From then on, I understood that that church and those people were never going to allow me to be who I was. And those people meant my parents too because they were so much part of that community. So I began my exit strategy. The church and my family had encouraged a duplicitous way of life—speaking one thing, doing another. It was a double standard. I had my driver's license and said I was never going back. My parents encouraged me to find another Church of Christ. Indeed, I located a kinder community. But it just happened to be next door to an Episcopal church. So I started going there instead, leaving the bulletin of the Church of Christ in the back of the car to let my parents think that that was where I had been."

One day the Episcopal rector introduced himself and, to Davey's amazement, asked if he had joined the church because he was gay. The rector made it clear that there was a place for him at God's table as well as a place in the parish community. "I didn't come out to him but I felt so alive and welcomed," said Davey. "He let me get involved in the community and gave me an entrance I had been missing in the Church of Christ. I was seventeen and became an acolyte. This, in fact, led to my first relationship with another altar server, an innocent kiss in the sacristy and an embracing understanding of what this meant for me."

When, as a student of international economics, Davey went to college in Kalamazoo, Michigan, he was able to be openly gay and passionately Christian in an Episcopal faith community. It was a three-and-a-half-hour drive from home and he knew his parents were unlikely to make any surprise visits. Soon he was involved in a gay group on campus, exploring short-term and longer-term relationships and discovering plenty of role models in the church that led him to conclude that being gay and spiritual were not mutually exclusive.

Davey had still not come out to his parents. When he eventually did, at the age of twenty, he had to tell them twice "because the first time it didn't stick." A relationship had just broken up dramatically, and he had called his parents late one evening, saying he was coming home as he needed to get away from college for a while. Returning tearfully in the early hours, he knew his parents would want to know why he was so upset. This would be the moment of truth. His father met him in the garage and said, "Don't say anything that might shock your mother." But he did. Sitting in front of the fireplace with the television on mute—"it was always on in our house"—he told them that a gay relationship at university had just ended and it wasn't his first. He said he needed them to understand, accept, and believe in him. It was a courageous request from an only child. Davey's parents presented him with two choices: either he could go back to college and find a therapist who could talk him out of his inclination or he could stay at home with them and seek counseling nearby. In the end they located a local Bible-based therapist who, to Davey's surprise, was completely understanding of his predicament, giving him the freedom to be who he was. He continued his college studies until graduation, then deliberately moved far away to Boston on the East Coast.

Working as an international student adviser at Harvard, Davey read for a master's degree in public administration. He was out in his workplace. Of the seventy colleagues in his office, twelve were men; eleven of them were gay. There was a large gay and lesbian staff organization at Harvard—hundreds of men and women who would meet every Thursday afternoon for conversation and lunch in one of the conference rooms.

"I was able to see that I could be gay, in a job and have legitimacy," Davey continued, "but I was still missing a sympathetic Christian community. I hadn't found a church, someone to date, or gay friends who were open to my idea of spirituality and Christianity. While I was very happy, I was still very lonely."

So Davey satisfied his dual needs through Internet chat rooms where he connected with a cyber community which enabled him to discuss spiritual matters. He felt he was getting somewhere, but meeting people who would respect him specifically as a Christian proved the biggest challenge, more testing than the coming-out process.

"My nickname in the chat rooms was 'Saint Sergius.' People asked some alarming and skeptical questions about why a saint was in this gay chat room. But when I explained about how I felt, that God wasn't judging me for being gay and that there were plenty of ways to be Christian and gay, they began to ask a lot of questions. We started having long conversations about spirituality and theology. Others talked about their personal histories, raising a range of theological questions in return, ones they may not have dared ask elsewhere."

The Bible-based conversations about sexuality and spirituality burgeoned and the discussions often went on into the night. Davey's two worlds were coinciding in cyberspace, if not in reality. "It felt incredibly unnatural," he disclosed. "What I really wanted was a group of healthy people in my Boston church who were gay. I wanted them to be able to talk with me about normal day-to-day issues. Instead I found the gay people there were partnered already, wounded or unwilling to begin conversations that might lead to more intimate relationships. Some were so keen to talk about their sexuality that the spirituality languished.

"Time and again, both in Boston and later here in San Francisco, I concluded that gay people were all right with being gay and Christian, but they really wanted to be gay about it. Friends would tell me to go to a certain church because it was gay. I soon discovered it was the Friday and Saturday night crowd showing up on a Sunday, a little bleary-eyed and ready to get their spiritual fix before moving on to brunch in a gay bar. They were seeking gay churches and gay Christian meetings that were more about swapping phone numbers and going out on dates than any form of spiritual development. I am still searching for that healthy fusion. It makes me wonder about my own search. Perhaps I am searching for something that doesn't exist."

Davey said Holy Innocents' Episcopal Church in San Francisco fed him spiritually on many levels. It was multi-generational and diverse, with the right mix of straight and gay worshipers. It had led to his understanding that gayness was simply another facet of his personality rather than its defining feature. It was crucial to be part of a community and be himself, regardless of what that self really was. It was no big surprise when members of the church found out he was gay, but nobody cared either. "Gay" was never a label for him, and he valued the freedom he discovered in being able to lead Bible study classes without having to offer "the gay version" of the Scriptures. And he could sing in the choir without having to look at pictures of pop music's gay icons, Abba, that some young gay singers kept hidden under their hymn books. It was "a real community of love, tenderness and support." To Davey, it seemed like the Episcopal Church was naming homosexuality, acknowledging it and supporting it, even in places where it tended to be traditionally conservative.

Now Davey has put his computer skills to different use. He works for Every Voice Network, a global online community of Anglicans involved in social justice projects. It provides tools and resources for peace and justice education, the inclusive Gospel and curriculum development, along with opportunities for virtual and real-time discussions on spiritual and political issues of the day. Here, in touch with people gay and spiritual, Davey is communicating with a deeper community that had long been eluding him. He says he regards the network as a group of people who are able to process painful issues in public forms—"a place echoing with voices of every kind."

On the other hand, Davey accepts it is often difficult for any community of faith, based on literalism, to see legitimacy, spirituality, and goodness in all of God's creation, gays and lesbians included. He recently came across a rural fundamentalist church undergoing "some significant tension" because there were lesbians in the congregation. When one of the women came out, she and her partner were told to get out.

Even though Davey felt it had been absolutely right for him to close the fundamentalist chapters of his younger years, the church of his upbringing had nonetheless been a community of people "doing what they were doing because they felt called to do it that way." They had been misguided—he had read enough books on theology, spirituality and sexuality to point out the flaws in their judgment. But at the end of the day they were not really flaws at all. That was what they had believed. He could never hate or be angry with them for that. He felt compassion and hoped they might embrace a broader vision one day. "I resent some of the ways they went about teaching, but not about the passion of their message," he said.

Davey did not deny that his fundamentalist background might have alienated some potential partners and could account for the fact that he was still single. Finding the right person was essentially about love and companionship. "When I love someone, I can't distinguish between loving their spirit, loving their body and loving their mind," he said. "All that God has given me—intellect, body and spirit—are the very attributes I have to offer the community and the people I want to be intimate with." He spoke also of the "incredible joy" he had discovered in some of his platonic friendships, a spiritual and emotional intimacy never achieved with someone he had considered his boyfriend or partner at various times. "I don't rule that out as a way of living," he went on. "I derive a great deal of comfort, love and affection from that. I think those are legitimate relationships. I also believe many forms of intimacy are legitimate in the eyes of God. I haven't found myself feeling separated from God when I am in a sexual relationship. I don't drift apart. There isn't a single book or person with all the answers. The answers, and the abundance and generosity that go with them, reside inside us.

"Gay men and lesbians are forced by society to look at themselves with so many different lenses and this can lead to a deeper awareness of their spiritual selves as they become more whole individuals, integrating body, mind and spirit. I can't imagine what it is like to live your soul apart from your body and apart from your mind. I may have grown up in a religious environment where everything was black and white but I have come to appreciate that being gay and spiritual is a more colorful journey—and a much deeper one too."

twenty-four

On Being a Person

"I think the really important issue for gay people," reflected James Alison, "is not gay theology but Christian theology worked out with honesty from a gay perspective, starting from where one is. A gay theology, as such, sounds a little limiting. It suggests people are going round and round in circles over certain Bible texts and church teachings. It's really not about that. The point of the Christian faith is that one is loved as one is, starting from where one is."

I tracked down the globetrotting writer in Scotland, where he was giving a lecture in the shadow of Edinburgh Castle. It was unusual to find him on British soil, for his e-mails are usually dispatched from a basic Internet café in a remote part of the world. Born in London, James has studied, worked, and lived throughout Mexico, South America, and the United States. Charming, and a skilled mimic, he has an uncanny way of sounding both completely traditional and utterly revolutionary at the same time. He is the author of several extraordinary books, including *Knowing Jesus, Faith Beyond Resentment* and *On Being Liked*—difficult in many ways to get into but utterly enthralling once you pick up their unique rhythm. The Archbishop of Canterbury, Rowan Williams, is one of his many admirers, recommending him as "one of the freshest and most interesting" living writers on religion and theology.

According to Alison, the underlying question is not "Why are there so many homosexuals in the church?" but "Why does God love gay people so much?" God calls all people to love vulnerably—"and naturally, some of those who find themselves called into loving vulnerably are gay people. Because they often have to start from a vulnerable patch, perhaps loving in this way is easier for them."

Whether theologians are at liberty to express an opinion contrary to the church's position depends entirely on their employment safety. As a Catholic priest and theologian, living outside a religious order, Alison is "absolutely free" to discuss the issue. What he has had to learn is "proper responsibility and proper faithfulness" to the Word of God as he perceives it through the teaching of the Catholic Church. Other theologians might want to follow suit but often feel inhibited from voicing their true feelings because of the threat of losing their jobs. They would risk being considered to have stepped over the boundary in areas the church deemed "too hot to handle."

Alison, who became aware of his gay orientation at the age of nine, told me that for many homosexuals there came a phase when it was important for them to be able to claim and cling onto what might be termed "a gay identity." But it would be stultifying for them to remain there. It was essential, at some stage, for homosexuals to bring together the words "I" and "Am" and "Gay," he said. It was usually a relief for gay people to be in touch with who they were, when the burden of leading "a double, triple or quadruple life" could be finally lifted. What they then needed to discover was that the world was much larger and richer—and much less simplistic.

He considers it too easy for people to describe the Catholic Church as an organization of repressed homosexuals. "It's an immense body, existing in many different cultures where phases of life and self-understanding are worked out in different ways," he said. "In Zimbabwe, for example, homosexuality is becoming an issue, as it is already in various parts of South America where I have lived and worked. The notion of gayness is manifestly present in Latin America and has become part of the Spanish and Portuguese language, although one still shouldn't be fooled because in those places its meaning is often slightly different from what English people think it means.

"Some young gay men still move into the Catholic priesthood in Europe and North America. It is possible they might be consciously repressing their sexuality out of fear or feeling under pressure in their late twenties because they have not yet found a girlfriend," he postulated. "In the past, joining a religious order was often a safe option, although that trend is diminishing. Vocations are fewer. Both the church authorities and gay people are discovering that joining a celibate male order is not the 'only way' to exist as gay. Up to forty years ago, the church was one of the safest places to be gay in an extremely unsafe society—and one of the most liberal places. What has moved on has been the idea of coming out. Now that people are able to come out, it suddenly makes the clerical world seem a very oppressive place. But it is important to remember that for a whole generation of people, now in their seventies, one of the safest places to be gay was within monastery walls."

Alison doesn't dispute the suggestion that both gay and straight people, who are called to public ministry can use their office as a disguise to a lesser or greater extent. "For as long as there are uniforms, there will be substitutes for the hard work of being a person," he told me. "But that's not necessarily to be despised. For most of us, disguises of one sort or another are necessary in order to provide a space to grow into. I'm hesitant about condemning them—but we should be encouraged to move beyond our masks."

But, as he carefully pointed out, the disguise is not essentially related to the uniform. It is connected with the discourse. The uniform can be a more or less "absurd form of camp," but the discourse—what people actually say—is more serious. Regardless of one's sexuality, one of the temptations of religious people in particular is to avoid self-implicatory speech, to talk objectively about "them," but not to be able to say "I." This becomes more evident for homosexuals because of the inherent temptation to talk about gay people as "they," even if that person happens to be one of them. "I have seen it again and again in the clerical life where there is clearly a very strong temptation to talk about *they*. It is a means by which people think they are being helpful by saying nice things about "them"—without allowing the word "I" to emerge. Many straight people also find it difficult to be self-implicatory without being self-obsessed when talking of the things of God. Homiletic training in seminaries does not encourage people to descend into the painful places of talking from the vulnerable position of someone who is loved, feels unloved or is trying to discover what it is to be loved."

A religious order, for example, is a community of disparate people trying to move beyond specific coexistence into "something a bit more real" but there are still masks. "No one as far as I know has come up with a recipe for automatic authenticity," he said, laughing. "I don't think one ought to imagine that the religious communities are very different from any other group of people, except that they tend to be total societies. There, individuals are entirely dependent on one another. On the other hand, people who work in offices but live somewhere else are not totally dependent on those they associate with during the day. A religious order functions within total enclosure. There is therefore a slightly more intense 'hothouse atmosphere' which also means that defensiveness can go deeper."

Alison admitted ruefully that community life had saved him from feeling that he had to kill himself at one stage. "It was the only port in the storm and a very good port and I am very grateful to it. It proved so good for me that eventually I had to move on. Eventually the very same forces that had made me safe made me unsafe for it. There are certain sorts of honesty that are not easily handled in communities that are not communities of choice. The members haven't chosen each other and you can be dangerous to it by being honest in certain sorts of ways, and maybe it is uncharitable to insist."

What Alison thinks is "clearly idolatrous" about the gay debate in the Catholic Church is the idea that homosexuality is a "make-or-break" issue. "Only in a completely topsy-turvy church could something as relatively unimportant as sexual identity come to be a touchstone issue," he observed. "Curiously, I rather think that the Vatican has worked out that it is a third-order truth. It couldn't and shouldn't be an issue destructive of the gift of faith, the gift of communion or of the possibility of being a priest or religious. Whatever the truth about this issue—and we're all in discovery—the one thing I think we should be agreed on is that *it's not terribly important*. Once we realize this, we can move on. If it's not terribly important, people oughtn't to be kicked out of communities because of it."

For James Alison, all his books and lectures are "honest attempts to converse about the things of God from the position of someone who is trying to work out what it is to be a priest and a gay man living under a particular set of cultural circumstances but at the same time a person who is attempting to follow the Gospel, blessing those who curse him and loving those who hate him. That is the only way gay people can be free—by not living in reaction to what was done to them. It is the emotional equivalent of going the second mile. Unfortunately, for whatever reasons of fear, and with some exceptions, the good shepherds in all our Christian churches have run away from this particular wolf and seem to have refused to feed their sheep. They are too frightened to, so some of us have to try to feed the sheep instead.

"The issue is not (and never has been) about same-sex practice. It is about violence being dressed up as the Word of God. That was something that *had* to be fought against. That is why our identity is secondary, because it has been formed by our dealing with that violence. The issue is about how we set ourselves and each other free from idols."

The need for gay people to justify themselves religiously seemed especially strong in Protestant cultures, even though in theory those were strong on "justification through faith," Alison explained. Although raised in just such a culture, he had spent a lot of time living in traditionally Catholic countries with more Mediterranean attitudes and had found that "it's not quite like that in those places—you don't need to justify things in the same way." He went on, "A huge amount of literature that one finds in religious bookstores in Britain is yet another attempt to make the Bible sound friendly. That's odd, but it's also part of the culture. That's how the other side works as well. It's natural enough that the first response of weak people is to try to fight back with the weapons of the people who are fighting against them. As you grow strong, you realize that you don't need to fight back. You need to get on with living your life and doing what is right."

twenty-five

The Beat of
a Different Drum

"I suppose we're like a suburban family," said Julian as he took me on a guided tour of Manchester's gay neighborhood. "For many people, it's a means of escape, a place where they can go and be themselves.

Julian is a twenty-four-year-old music student, singer, and songwriter who is aiming high for a career in the British record industry. To make ends meet he has a part-time job as a waiter in one of the village's popular gay venues where loud pulsations and lonely hearts clash discordantly in the smoky light.

He pointed out the various locations where the cult British television series *Queer as Folk* had been filmed. At certain times of the year, the bar-laden street beside the canal is teeming with young, middle-aged, and old partygoers alike. But, as the TV series itself illustrated, sometimes these are vulnerable people, drawn to the area in search of love and belonging, tempted by what others regard as an illusory form of hedonistic bliss.

"*Queer as Folk* opened with the main character sitting out on the canal wall over there," he indicated. "He was only fifteen and had never been out on his own before. You do see that look in people's eyes. They venture down here on their own because they haven't told people they are gay. It's desperation on their part to make friends. It does look very lonely. You want to reach out your hand to them but you can't be friends to everyone in that role. Any form of contact could be misinterpreted. You talk to some people to be friendly but then you find the regulars will talk to you all the time. You cannot be friends with everyone. I try to smile at people and say 'Hi' but then people want to get to know you. I feel sorry for them but I don't feel they really want to get to *know* you. They just want the contact with a gay person.

"It can be unwelcoming. People will look at you if you are amusing or are taking drugs or have a sexy body, but unless you have some sexual appeal they might not be interested in you. Managers of gay bars tend to employ only good-looking people as a means of attracting gay customers to a sexualized culture centered round drinking.

"Some of the bars attract older people on their own. They just seem to stand there for the whole night. They must hate the music. You see them trying to tap to the rhythm with their feet. They stand in the same place every night. Some don't socialize with anyone. One man just sits at the bar, dipping his beard in his pint. I often wonder what is going on in his mind. Then there are men who just sit scribbling things down on bits of paper. I sometimes wonder if they are going to go home and kill themselves."

Julian said he was sensitive to the isolation of other people because his own homosexuality once propelled him toward the brink. He was brought up as a strong-minded individualist in an isolated part of the British Isles. His mother had entered a Roman Catholic religious order as a young woman and lived as a nun for six years before opting for a less enclosed life. She left the convent, studied at university, and eventually married. Over the years, however, she lost her faith and no longer believes in God. Julian said he had gone to Mass with his mother as a ten-year-old but had never been forced to attend. He would like to believe but these days fatalism had replaced any faith he might once have had. He told me that, as he had been born gay, he was never likely to feel welcome in the Christian church, which was "completely out of touch with the reality of young people's lives."

Always sensing "something different" about him, Julian hung around with girls at primary school but knew he was not sexually attracted to the opposite sex. Confirmation of his gay identity came at the age of eleven while he was watching a film in which two men were kissing. "I lay in bed and just cried because I realized that was who I was," he explained. "But I decided to keep it a secret." Nonetheless, because Julian was, by his own admission, effeminate at school, he was always the target of gay bullying. He said he was hit twice and was repeatedly taunted as a "poof" ("fag") as he walked between lessons every day. It seemed that everyone in the school was against him. Like Daniel, whose story was told earlier in the book, such was his sense of fear that, to this day, he felt he could never walk alone through the streets of his hometown in case a former pupil recognized and "battered" him. The taunts followed him from primary school through the secondary system and into the sixth form, when he eventually decided to come out at the age of sixteen. He decided to hold his head high, and many who had always shouted "poof, poof, poof" had come up to him and said, "Well done, mate, for admitting it." Julian went on, "In some ways the bullying carried on, but I was definitely glad I had done it. I can understand why people don't come out at school. It is very difficult. Lots of my fellow pupils were gay but they wouldn't admit it, even though it was obvious to me. Having said that, when you come out, you are still on your own and don't know how others will react to you. I could not have left coming out much longer than I did. It was such a relief when I could start saying who I liked and behaving as heterosexuals do. It was an amazing feeling the first time I did it."

But Julian's path toward self-acceptance and authenticity was paved with psychological difficulties. In his early teenage years, he thought about killing himself and, at the age of fourteen, once attempted suicide by taking an overdose. He told his parents that he had wanted to end it because he hated his father. But that hadn't really been true, he confessed. His suicide attempt had been directly related to his being gay, especially the problems that had emerged from his growing self-awareness. "It was about the loneliness, the isolation, the fact that I could never tell anyone anything real about myself and that I was living a lie all the time," he said. "I didn't have anyone to turn to. I was very shy. A couple of years later I phoned a gay helpline, met a couple of people, and that's when I decided to come out. It was my salvation. Some people live a complete lie all their life, never doing anything they want to do in terms of relationships. If I hadn't come out when I did, I wouldn't be living the life I am now where all my friends know me as gay and it doesn't matter."

Being openly gay has undoubtedly made Julian more confident and positive. Living in denial would have resulted in greater insecurities. He always worried that, if he came out, he would be rejected by his family, friends, or wider society. That hasn't proved to be the case. "I think wearing masks can be very damaging. It's bad if the majority of your life is a lie. You can spend your whole time tortured up in a ball trying to rationalize, justify or change yourself. I know people who are completely out but their parents don't know. I needed my parents to know. My mum was fine. She thought I was going to have a hard life but now she realizes I am not. My dad is very old fashioned."

After going to university, Julian began to mix with others as an openly gay man. He acknowledges that the way he initially acted and perceived the gay dimension of himself was shallow. Self-obsession took hold and, on the dance-floor, he was deluded into believing he was greatly admired. But coming out so young has enabled him to embrace his femininity and not be ashamed of it. "As the token gay in the flat and by working in a gay bar you do lose your defenses. I spent all my life trying to be more masculine and less feminine. Now I accept the fact that the way I act is feminine. I think femininity is about being in touch with your emotions and being able to deal with them better, not being afraid to hug or kiss someone, being able to be more intimate with people without as many barriers."

Julian says he is more comfortable with *himself* now that he does not have to "act, sit or talk in a socially acceptable way." He has no hesitation in hugging friends, whereas at school he dared not take the risk. There was always something holding him back and preventing him from doing what he most desired. "When you are comfortable with yourself, you are more yourself, more likeable and loveable. I think people who do not own themselves become defensive, put barriers up, won't allow themselves to like people and prevent others from liking them. I think so-called modern man, which people often talk about, is not unlike the gay man—someone who is more in touch with his feminine side. Women are more in touch with their masculine sides these days. They don't have to conform to a particular gender. Although we are all of one gender, I don't think that every part of our personalities is or should be set by that gender."

Himself no stranger to victimization, Julian told me how appalled and moved he had been by the murder of Matthew Shepard, a gentle and compassionate American student who was savagely beaten to death in 1998 because he was gay. The twenty-one-year-old, who had served as an acolyte in the Episcopal Church, had been lured from a campus bar shortly after midnight by two men who pretended they were gay. He was driven to a remote area, tied to a fence, tortured, beaten and pistol-whipped by his attackers while he begged for his life. He was then left for dead in near freezing temperatures. When a cyclist discovered Matthew eighteen hours later, he initially mistook him for a scarecrow. He was unconscious and suffering from hypothermia. According to one report, "his face was caked with blood except where it had been partially washed clean by tears." Matthew died in hospital with his family at his bedside. As an article at the time put it:

> Matthew was killed to make a point. His fragile, broken body was left strung up like an animal as a clear message to gay men everywhere. How can someone be so consumed with hatred for a fellow human being that atrocities like this happen? Why is homosexuality even an issue? Why does it excite such feelings of hatred and violence in people, when their lives will never be touched by it? Why is a person's sexuality anyone else's business; and who are we to judge other people?
>
> Part of the answer, at least, lies in a culture that ridicules gay men, and dehumanizes them, so that their lives are seen to have less value. It starts with verbal taunts in the school playground, and leads to the persecution of people because of their sexual orientation. There is a climate of hatred in society which encourages murderers to act. This was a hate crime, and Matthew was brutally attacked, and left there to bleed his life away, simply because of who he was."[1]

Julian said he had been shocked to learn that, at Matthew's funeral in Casper, Wyoming, a hard-line evangelical had turned up with members of his church to protest, not against the attack, but against Matthew himself. They held signs declaring "God Hates Fags" and "Matt in Hell." "I thought that was disgusting—I couldn't believe those homophobic feelings were still out there, especially among people who would class themselves as Christian," he said. "These views alienate me further and further from religion which can clearly be used to oppress and persecute. I could not believe that the minister felt he was doing the work of God."

He applauded, however, the work of the Matthew Shepard Foundation, set up by Matthew's parents, Dennis and Judy Shepard. The non-profit-making organization is carrying out Matthew's legacy by developing educational materials and programs and supporting projects, activities and documentaries that raise awareness of the issues surrounding discrimination and diversity. Its mission statement speaks of the need to establish environments where young gay people can feel safe and be themselves. Its goal is "to replace hate with understanding, compassion and acceptance."

Were he ever to believe in God, Julian said he would find himself in "an awkward predicament" because he would instinctively want to be challenging people in the church who held such views. So even if he were religious, he would still be in a dilemma. He did not have much respect for the church because of its tendency to oppress gay people.

When gay friends he had known a long time suddenly came out spiritually and admitted they believed in God, it shocked him. It was hard for him to accept that openly homosexual people like himself could dare believe in God. "I look at the coverage in the newspapers about Christian reactions to homosexuality and cannot believe what I am reading," he said.

"I might be inspired by Roman Catholicism if I felt it supported gay people in their loneliness. But I don't think it does. The church goes on about no sex before marriage but I think I would be more attracted to Catholicism if gay people could get married in the eyes of the church. That would be about making a commitment to another person before God. Why should the church be against that? Perhaps it just doesn't feel comfortable with the idea of two men lying beside each other. I don't think I would be ready for such a marriage yet but I have these romantic notions from time to time about being swept off my feet one day. I think I do want to love—and have somebody to love me."

twenty-six

A Gay Priest in Hollywood

As I entered the grounds of The Abbey in the suburbs of Los Angeles, I noticed first the reflection of a cross silhouetted against the courtyard wall. Then I spied a grey stone statue of St. Francis. I watched as visitors came up and touched the saint with such affection he could have been real. Inside was a statue of Jesus holding a child and another of the Virgin Mary with arms outstretched. Around her mouth I detected the imprint of lipstick, left by devotees who had obviously kissed as they passed by. As I ambled further into the building, I saw burning candles and a large rusted steel crucifix of Christ the Redeemer.

But this was not a Californian monastery on the edge of an American city. The Abbey is one of West Hollywood's most fashionable gay venues, frequented by a host of stars. Its religious symbolism, I learned, brought comfort to lesbians and gay men alienated from the church. A form of folk religion, perhaps, or is it that those who come here have distant memories of a religious past?

In a glitzy world of inner uncertainty, the saint clearly offers a sense of security. "You see our gay customers giving Francis a drink or a cigarette," said an assistant manager who told me that he had been married nine years before he could own his homosexuality. "Gay people have been hurt so many times they are afraid of being wounded again. They try to put up very tall walls to fortify themselves against vulnerability and they have a tendency to create personas to protect themselves. Most of our bartenders are film actors. For some, working here is a step on the way out because in the studios they have to put up pretence of being straight if they want to hold on to their jobs."

A few miles away in Hollywood itself, close to the Kodak Theatre, where the Oscars are awarded, lies Saint Thomas the Apostle Episcopal Church, whose mission is "to be a holy place where love is found, where all are named and where hearts are freed to change the world." About ninety percent of the congregation is lesbian or gay. They work mostly in the film industry as actors, producers, directors, production assistants, broadcasters, lawyers, fundraisers, and real estate agents.

A former rector, Father Carroll Barbour, was among the first priests in Los Angeles to be involved in the gay community. At the height of the AIDS pandemic, when clergy could find themselves conducting two funerals a week, St. Thomas's became known as the church where everyone was welcome. Its respect for homosexuals has made a long and lasting impression on the gay community. There is much good will around because of the church's commitment. On the altar of the Damian Chapel, with its icon of Saint Damian the leper, patron saint of people with HIV/AIDS, lies a large memorial book containing the names of ten thousand people from around the world. All have died from AIDS-related illnesses. The book began to be compiled in the early 1980s and names are still being added. Every week, at the Thursday evening Mass, up to sixty people (a page of names) are remembered. The church also has an outreach program for the homeless and runs three twelve-step programs every day for those who have dependent or obsessive behavior associated with recovering from addictions to alcohol, drugs, eating and sex.

The current rector, Father Ian Elliott Davies, is a Welshman who left the Anglo-Catholic parish of All Saints, London, in 2002 to take up the position. One of his references was Jeffrey John. Ian, who is regarded as a fine preacher, was, in fact, headhunted. And far from presenting itself as a difficulty, a homosexual orientation was almost at the top of the list of desired attributes on the job description. The Bishop of Los Angeles, Jon Bruno, was prepared to appoint a gay or a straight priest. But he insisted that if the new rector were homosexual, he would have to be open about it. There could be no double standards.

The transition had far-reaching consequences for Ian personally because when he came out to California, he also came out as a gay priest. "Saint Thomas the Apostle was almost made for me and I was made for it," he told me. "Every experience in my life has prepared me in one way or another for the kind of work I do here. Every failure I have faced in my life, every type of disappointment I have ever known, has made me who I am today, helping me to understand, sympathize and be involved in all kinds of issues here.

"I would never be ashamed to call myself gay now. In the American church, the Bishop of Los Angeles supports me and expects me to be faithful to the message of the Gospel. But I have no fear of describing myself as gay, a Christian and a priest. This is the affirmative action of God's good grace. I have a passion for the people. I love them. My care and my concern for them form the overriding focus of my ministry."

Along with San Francisco, Hollywood and West Hollywood were probably the most liberated and integrated areas of the United States for the lesbian, gay, bisexual and transgender community, Ian explained. There had been a long history of tolerance in Los Angeles, where many city council members and police officers were themselves gay. The annual Christopher Street West Parade through the two-mile Santa Monica Boulevard, ending in West Hollywood, had become a major gay and lesbian march. In 2003 the Diocese of Los Angeles was the biggest single group represented. It was led by Bishop Bruno sitting at the front of the float. A straight man, Bishop Bruno is a six-foot, four-inch former professional football player and policeman, generous-hearted and big-spirited, said Ian. Keen to affirm everyone in the church, the bishop's presence was seen as a sign of reconciliation between the church and the gay community. As a result, St. Thomas's receives many new visitors every year.

Chatting to me in his clerical suit, over a Saturday lunchtime salad in a gay restaurant, where he was clearly popular with the waiters, Ian pointed out that, while it could be taken for granted that many of the other diners were gay, you wouldn't automatically assume they were all Christian. Yet many sitting around us were in fact his parishioners. "People who have known each other for years in the gay community sometimes have to come out to their friends as being Christian," he said. "While I eat in gay restaurants, I don't go out to the gay bars. This is not because I believe it is wrong but because I would see a huge number of my parishioners. I don't want to be in situations where they could get mixed signals or whatever. I do, in fact, have a significant relationship. I get on extremely well with my partner, Matthew, who shares the rectory with me. He is someone I can relax and unwind with. Being gay isn't really about the big area of debate—sex. It's about waking up in the morning and having a cup of tea with the person you love. It's about sharing the most ordinary, boring, dull, few minutes of the morning with the person that makes you *you*."

Ian thought the danger for Hollywood's gay community, especially its Christian members, was that on Wednesdays they tended to go to the gay restaurant, on Thursdays to the gay bank, on Fridays to the gay supermarket, and on Saturdays to the gay cinema. Then on Sunday they went to their gay church. That was how the community could become a ghetto. The entire Hollywood culture was one of disposability, especially in terms of food, possessions, and relationships. People treated each other as consumer objects. Moreover, West Hollywood was body beautiful. Everyone was "muscular, buff, tanned and good-looking." Ian reckoned there were probably more gyms per square mile than anywhere else in the United States. Rubbing shoulders with the movie sets, it was a world of image and illusion. And those who failed to match up to the standard, and lost out on work because of it, often felt obliged to change their physical appearance through cosmetic surgery.

The abuse of "crystal meth" (otherwise known as "ice," "speed," "crank" or "glass") was a problem of epidemic proportions for the area, Ian pointed out. Registered officially as methamphetamine, the white powder was a powerful stimulant for the nervous system. It could be snorted, smoked, injected, or swallowed. The drug caused an initial rush which the brain received as a reward. This was followed by a heightened state of awareness and agitation that could result in violent and erratic behavior.

Huge numbers of gay people used the drug to make sex more enjoyable. This had a devastating effect on their lives. People turned to crime to get money to pay for it. They no longer lived in the real world. "Just walking up and down Santa Monica Boulevard, you'll see people who are spaced out, not only the homeless, for whom heroin is also a huge problem, but also the more affluent members of the gay community. They have every luxury they could possibly want. It's almost as though people want to find a bigger thrill. Crystal meth is the drug of choice and it's so vicious. One parishioner I recently visited on a rehabilitation ward would very readily admit that he lacked direction in his life so he took crystal meth to give him some kind of kick. But it focused his attention solely on sex and how to get more of it. I think Saint Thomas's gives people an alternative to that, a reality rooted in the daily Mass as a rhythm and focus to their day. The church is there to provide a daily support network and to give people some guidance in their lives."

In so far as gay people had heard of the church, they certainly knew there was now a gay bishop, he said. People often opened conversations by commenting, "Oh, you're a priest from the church which has the gay bishop." Homosexuals in Hollywood felt there was somebody on their side. Most people who reflected on the issues sensibly would realize that being gay was almost as immaterial as whether someone was left- or right-handed. The church was an inclusive body, much larger than anyone's prejudices. There was an openness and an acceptance within local parish life which were good and healthy, but members of his congregation also included some who had been thrown out of their homes by their parents, who might have discovered a love letter and ordered their children on to the streets.

I wondered if, at this time in the church's history, Ian was relieved to be in Los Angeles rather than London. "The atmosphere in Britain is much more tense than it is here and the Church of England seems to be an unpleasant place to be," he replied. "This is somewhat ironic because the Church of England should be taking a long historical approach to the gay debate, regarding it as a small issue in its long history. For once it's the American church that's saying this is a small issue in the long history of the Christian tradition."

As Jeffrey John had supported Ian in his application to become rector of St. Thomas's, I asked if he had been in touch with the theologian since his withdrawal as Bishop of Reading. Ian told me he had sent cards of support, promising to pray for Jeffrey and to remember him at Mass. "I think the disturbing thing about Jeffrey John was that the appointment had gone through," said Ian. "He'd been nominated. His nomination had been accepted and it was then that objections largely from the evangelical wing started coming, notably from Asia and Africa. I find it bizarre that a suffragan appointment in the Diocese of Oxford should have become the litmus test for this issue and that what was a relatively minor appointment should have become a flashpoint for so many prejudices. There are still some very important questions to be asked here. How supported was he and how far did the external forces influence the internal politics?

"I can only guess at his feelings. He's a quiet man who would never choose to court controversy. What happened was one of the blots on the history of the Church of England. It is unthinkable that such a good and holy man, a superb thinker and a biblical scholar, should be chosen by a bishop and, we believe, appointed by God's good grace, then be made to withdraw."

Ian told me that, ever since his teenage years, when he had first become passionate about theology, the struggle to keep his sexuality and his spirituality harnessed and integrated had been constant. When he had first realized he was both gay and Christian, he had not wished to abandon one or the other. "We are called to be in relationship and that's a profoundly theological statement," he said. "It's all to do with the Trinity. Its roots are in the nature of the relationship between the Father, the Son and the Holy Spirit, and the mutually indwelling and fulfillment of each of those persons in the other. That is the paradigm for humanity, made in the image of God. In that sense, perhaps gay people, who know a great deal about relationships, how fragile they are and how they can fail, are able to teach the rest of the Body of Christ something about the nature of forgiveness, grace and healing. To take seriously Christ's injunction that we do unto others what we would have them do unto us means we sit down, listen and dialogue. We don't shout. We don't react like some evangelical protestors who spew vitriol and hate. We should listen to one another's prejudices and fears, and seek some kind of understanding, a mutual dialogue and reconciliation. Sometimes it's only when people have understood pain, hurt and wounds that they are able to forgive others as well as themselves. That's a difficult lesson to learn."

The theology of the cross was particularly inspiring in that respect. It concerned "the theology of the glory of God and the vulnerability of God's being—that God makes himself vulnerable to us." That, he felt, was good news in the early years of the twenty-first century, which was already being defined by power, strength, fighting, and standing up to the enemy. The Gospel message was precisely the opposite. God had put himself into the hands of his creation. He had made himself vulnerable to humanity. He yearned for us, loved us, desired us.

"I think being gay in Hollywood is about realizing one can be vulnerable without being attacked," said Ian. "I have no fear of being attacked in any way, shape or form here in California. There is something about the atmosphere here that is open. Perhaps I have learned more here about humanity, vulnerability and fragility. These are the very places where God is at work."

finale

A Symphony of Love

This book is dedicated to a Roman Catholic nun I feel particularly privileged to know. Sister Eva Heymann is not only a companion on the journey but a special friend, always compassionate, intuitive and wise. Born into a nominally Jewish family in Germany in 1927, she became a refugee in England, was received into the Catholic Church and later joined the Society of the Holy Child Jesus. A former teacher and psychiatric social worker, Eva spent ten years with the Terrence Higgins Trust, the first HIV/AIDS agency in Britain. She has also been a volunteer at the Mildmay Mission Hospital which supports people living with HIV/AIDS, as well as their friends and families. Eva has also assisted women and children seeking asylum and has long been involved in spiritual direction and retreat work.

"Homosexual people have been ostracized by those who call themselves the Body of Christ—yet it could only be in Christ's own identification with our woundedness that such a body could have meaning in the twenty-first century," she points out. "This is the woundedness of people who have been persecuted, rejected and, in many ways, maltreated—sometimes physically—because of their God-given sexuality. Eventually their suffering may bring some change in the attitudes of those who are afraid of the breadth, length and depth of God's love. The very label 'straight' implies that anyone who does not fit into that category is crooked or deformed. Yet God does not create in uniformity but in diversity, as we can see all around us in the beauty of nature."

The place of gay people at the margins, at the edge of the Body of Christ, has resonance with the stable in which the Christ-child was born, Eva senses. "The stable or cave, which sheltered animals, was inferior to the basic requirements offered to human beings. Christ was born in a desolate situation and it is often in the context of desolation that Christ begins his work in and through us, bringing out our hidden potential for creativity."

There is always hope, she feels, when people refuse to allow themselves to be incapacitated by other people's fears—and where they can be true to themselves before God. "The essence of the Gospel lies in love and redeemed suffering. In order to grow in Christ-likeness, one has to be open and vulnerable—with the totality of oneself."

Eva believes her work has enabled her to discern how God is present in every person. All of us face the same challenges to love and be loved—and to be faithful. She has witnessed "the most wonderful faithful relationships" in the gay community but has also observed many fraught situations in which women and men have been struggling with issues of friendship, fidelity and partners in much the same way as heterosexual people. Whether one is gay, straight, bisexual or transgender, she says, all of us are vulnerable human beings before God. The challenge is to use the gifts God has given for the good of others. Not to appreciate that reality or celebrate such uniqueness "would seem like a denial of the inclusiveness of God's love."

She knows of lesbian and gay people who choose not to have a sexual relationship, preferring a very close friendship. "Society as a whole would never believe such relationships were possible because the culture in which we live ridicules or denies it," she explains. "In this way society projects its own fears about sexuality on an outside group like the gay community. This is clearly a form of scapegoating. When we scapegoat somebody, we point one finger away from us and three fingers toward ourselves. Our fear of what other people think runs very deep inside us.

"When I told my mother I was going to be a nun, her immediate response was 'How am I going to tell my friends?' When somebody tells their parents, 'I'm gay,' a father might exclaim, 'My God, what are they going to say down the pub? Where have I failed?' This seems to reflect a deep-seated fear: that anyone who identifies closely with those who do not conform to accepted social